REVIVAL YEAR SERMONS, 1859

After an engraving by J Cochran

Yours very truly

C H Spurgeon

REVIVAL
YEAR
SERMONS

Preached at the
Surrey Gardens Music Hall during

1859

by
C. H. Spurgeon

*"The Lord our God be with us, as he was with our fathers: let
him not leave us nor forsake us."*—I KINGS viii. 57.

THE BANNER OF TRUTH TRUST

PRINTED IN GREAT BRITAIN BY
BILLING AND SONS LIMITED, GUILDFORD AND LONDON

"The old truth that Calvin preached, that Augustine preached, that Paul preached, is the truth that I must preach to-day, or else be false to my conscience and my God. I cannot shape the truth; I know of no such thing as paring off the rough edges of a doctrine. John Knox's gospel is my gospel. That which thundered through Scotland must thunder through England again."

"A dead calm is our enemy, a storm may prove our helper. Controversy may arouse thought, and through thought may come the Divine change."—C. H. SPURGEON.

CONTENTS

INTRODUCTION

THE year 1859 contained little of a political nature to make
it permanently memorable. The agony of the Crimean War
and the shock of the Indian Mutiny were over. The American
Civil War, with its repercussions on English trade, was yet to
come. Across the Channel the conflict between France and
Austria in the Italian peninsula was being fought without
English interference. Victoria Regina passed the twenty-
second year of her reign undisturbed, and in Westminster
Lord Palmerston began his comparatively uneventful second
ministry. But in the annals of the Christian Church this year
stands out significantly as a veritable year of grace. Such a
year Britain has not seen since, and its stirring episodes deserve lasting remembrance.

On a Tuesday evening, January 4th, 1859, twenty-four-year-
old Charles Haddon Spurgeon addressed a vast gathering, con-
vened by the Young Men's Christian Association, in the
Exeter Hall. *De Propaganda Fide* was his subject, and it led
him to plead the necessity of a revival: "We must confess
that, just now, we have not the outpouring of the Holy Spirit
that we could wish . . . Oh, if the Spirit of God should come
upon those assembled to-night, and upon all the assemblies of
the saints, what an effect would be produced! We seek not
for extraordinary excitements, those spurious attendants of
genuine revivals, but we do seek for the pouring out of the
Spirit of God . . . The Spirit is blowing upon our churches
now with His genial breath, but it is as a soft evening gale.
Oh, that there would come a rushing mighty wind, that should
carry everything before it! This is the lack of the times, the
great want of our country. May this come as a blessing from
the Most High!" The desire was fulfilled. In the spring of
1859, kindled by the news of the revival which began in
America in the winter of 1857-58, a widespread awakening
began in Northern Ireland and in Wales. In the early sum-
mer it spread from Ulster to Scotland, and by the end of the
year Spurgeon could write: "The times of refreshing from

9

the presence of the Lord have at last dawned upon our land."

Of all the preachers of that year of grace there was none more remarkably used than C. H. Spurgeon, and though London never became the centre of such revival scenes as were witnessed elsewhere, nevertheless there was no more influential voice in the whole land than that of the youthful pastor of New Park Street Chapel. Five years before, at the age of nineteen, he had left a small Baptist " cause " at Waterbeach, near Cambridge, to accept the pastorate of this London church.[1] It was a church that had fallen into serious decline. Not more than 200 people were meeting in a building designed for a congregation of 1,200. Within twelve months, however, the building was packed to capacity. By February, 1855, the enlargement of the old structure was an urgent necessity, and the congregation therefore moved to Exeter Hall (capable of holding 2,500-3,000) till the alterations were completed in May. But the enlargement of New Park Street Chapel was utterly inadequate, for by 1855 the whole of London had become aware of the new preacher in their midst. " Since the days of Wesley and Whitefield," reported the newspapers, " so thorough a religious furore has never existed." In June, 1856, the congregation was forced to return to the Exeter Hall for its evening services, and a fund was opened for a new building. In November a further move was necessary, and for three years the New Park Street Church met in the Surrey Gardens Music Hall on Sunday mornings. On successive Sundays throughout this period Spurgeon's gospel filled this great building with between 5,000 and 9,000 people! At the same time Spurgeon was generally preaching about ten times every week. By 1859 he had preached in Scotland, Ireland and much of England. He turned down pressing invitations to go to America, but his sermons were read widely there, and indeed in many parts of the world.

It was abundantly evident, therefore, that the power of the

---

[1] Spurgeon was born at Kelvedon, Essex, on June 19th, 1834. His conversion took place in January, 1850. He first preached at New Park Street in December, 1853, and was offered the pastorate, which he accepted, in April, 1854. With this congregation he remained till his death.

Holy Spirit was present in Spurgeon's ministry long before 1859. At the end of that revival year he wrote in the Preface of the fifth volume of *The New Park Street Pulpit:* "In the midst of these new displays of divine love, it is very pleasant to see the spots which have long been favoured retaining their wonted fruitfulness and rejoicing with joy unspeakable in progressing prosperity. Such is the case with the Church to which these sermons were addressed from the pulpit. Her bow abides in strength . . . For six years the dew has never ceased to fall, and the rain has never been withheld." Yet, Spurgeon continues: "At this time the converts are more numerous than heretofore, and the zeal of the church groweth exceedingly." Undeniably, even in his ministry, it was a remarkable year.

Perhaps one or two events stand out. On March 1st he preached to an overflowing congregation at Whitefield's Tabernacle. On July 10th, following upon the death of a man by lightning on Clapham Common, Spurgeon preached there in the open air to 10,000 people on "Be ye also ready." Two days later he preached to another open-air gathering at Rowland's Castle in a valley near Havant. Here the very hills took up the sound of his voice and the breathless congregation could hear his moving exhortation coming back and echoing away in the distance—"Come, Come, Come, Come!" The same month, on July 20th, Spurgeon preached in Wales for the first time, again in the open air, to a congregation of between 9,000-10,000. The inhabitants of Castleton, the village between Newport and Cardiff where this took place, had cause to remember the event till their dying day.

Such open-air meetings in country districts were a common feature of Spurgeon's ministry at this time. Even as late as October in 1859 we find him preaching in the open to a gathering of 4,000 at Carlton in Bedfordshire.

Spurgeon's last year in the Surrey Gardens Music Hall was 1859. For a certain time the owners had been deterred from opening the grounds and Hall on Sundays for entertainment by Spurgeon's intimation that the congregation would then cease to use the building. A valuable rent would thus be lost. But at length, hoping to gain more by their entertainment programme, they forced Spurgeon to act upon his word. Hence the Farewell Sermon included in this book. In fact, after this, the Music Hall " both morally and financially sank hopelessly," and was destroyed by fire in June, 1861. Many years later a hearer wrote the following impressions of those last services in the Music Hall : " I shall never forget the sermon on July 17th, 1859, ' The Story of God's Mighty Acts.' How he revelled in preaching that morning! It was very hot, and he kept on wiping the perspiration from his forehead; but his discomfort did not affect his discourse, his words flowed on like a torrent of sacred eloquence. . . . I was present at the last service held in the Music Hall, on December 11th, 1859. It was very foggy, but the place was crowded, as much indeed as it could be. I had a front seat in the second gallery, and therefore enjoyed a splendid view of the people. Mr. Spurgeon preached an earnest sermon on declaring the whole counsel of God. There is always something sad about last things; and, as I came away, I felt that one of the happiest experiences of my youth belonged to the past. So also—in my opinion— passed away the most romantic stage even in Mr. Spurgeon's wonderful life."

The sermons included in this book were all preached at the Surrey Music Hall and are typical of many preached there. In them will be found the cause of the phenomenal success which attended his ministry. What was it that gathered and held a congregation of some 8,000 people? Was it advertisement, bright services, musical accompaniments, counselling rooms and follow-up work? No, Spurgeon had none of these things! " Surely," says someone, " it was just the Gospel preached as it is everywhere preached to-day." It was the Gospel, but is it the same Gospel that prevails in so much of the evangelism of to-day? Let the reader of these sermons, with all seriousness, consider this for himself.

The strength of Spurgeon's ministry lay in his theology. He rediscovered what the Church had largely forgotten—the evangelistic power of so-called " Calvinistic " doctrine. In his speech on the laying of the foundation stone of his future Metropolitan Tabernacle, on August 15th, 1859, Spurgeon declared what was already generally known : " We believe in the five great points commonly known as Calvinistic. We look upon them as being five great lights which radiate from the cross of Christ."[1]   At the opening of the Tabernacle in 1861, addresses were given on these five points—Election, Human Depravity, Particular Redemption, Effectual Calling, The Final Perseverance of Believers.[2]   Far from being a hindrance to evangelism, Spurgeon looked upon these truths as the driving force of a Gospel ministry. "Election, I take it—and I am here speaking of the whole set of truths which group around this as their central sun—has not only a salting power, but exercises a flavouring and seasoning power over all our other doctrines.   The purest evangelism springs from this truth. . . .   The doctrine which looks at first as though it would hush every exertion with indolence, and make men sit down with listlessness and despair, is really the trump of God to awake the dead.   Because it honours God, God will honour it."

Moreover, Spurgeon saw a vital connection between the proclamation of these truths and the outbreak of revivals. " In the history of the Church, with but few exceptions, you could not find a revival at all that was not produced by the orthodox faith.   What was that great work which was done by Augustine, when the Church suddenly woke up from the pestiferous and deadly sleep into which Pelagian doctrine had cast it? What was the Reformation itself but the waking up of men's minds to those old truths?   However far modern Lutherans may have turned aside from their ancient doctrines, and I must confess some of them would not agree with what I now say, yet, at any rate, Luther and Calvin had no dispute about Predestination.   Their views were identical, and Luther's *Bondage Of The Will* is as strong a book upon the free grace of God as Calvin himself could have written.   Hear that great thunderer while he cries in that book: ' Let the Christian reader know, then, that God foresees nothing in a contingent manner; but that he foresees, proposes and acts from his eternal and unchangeable will.   This is the thunder stroke which breaks and overturns Free Will.'   Need I mention to you better names than Huss, Jerome of Prague, Farel, John

[1] *The Life and Work of C. H. Spurgeon*, by G. Holden Pike, Vol. II, p. 315.
[2] *The New Park Street and Metropolitan Tabernacle Pulpit*, Vol. VII, pp. 304-28.

Knox, Wickliffe, Wishart and Bradford?   Need I do more
than say that these held the same views, and that in their day
anything like an Arminian revival was utterly unheard of and
undreamed of.   And then, to come to more modern times,
there is the great exception, that wondrous revival under Mr.
Wesley, in which the Wesleyan Methodists had so large a
share; but permit me to say, that the strength of the doctrine
of Wesleyan Methodism lay in its Calvinism.   The great body
of the Methodists disclaimed Pelagianism, in whole and in
part.   They contended for man's entire depravity, the necessity for the direct agency of the Holy Spirit, and that the first
step in the change proceeds not from the sinner, but from
God.   They denied at the time that they were Pelagians.   Does
not the Methodist hold as firmly as ever we do, that man is
saved by the operation of the Holy Ghost, and the Holy Ghost
only?   And are not many of Mr. Wesley's sermons full of that
great truth, that the Holy Ghost is necessary to regeneration?
Whatever mistakes he may have made, he continually
preached the absolute necessity of the new birth by the Holy
Ghost, and there are some other points of exceedingly close
agreement; for instance, even that of human inability.   It
matters not how some may abuse us, when we say man could
not of himself repent or believe; yet, the old Arminian stan-
dards said the same.   True, they affirm that God has given
grace to every man, but they do not dispute the fact, that apart
from that grace there was no ability in man to do that which
was good in his own salvation.   And then, let me say, if you
turn to the continent of America, how gross the falsehood, that
Calvinistic doctrine is unfavourable to revivals.   Look at that
wondrous shaking under Jonathan Edwards, and others which
we might quote.   Or turn to Scotland—what shall we say of
M'Cheyne?   What shall we say of those renowned Calvinists,
Dr. Chalmers, Dr. Wardlaw, and before them Livingstone,
Haldane, Erskine and the like?   What shall we say of the men
of their school, but that, while they held and preached un-
flinchingly the great truths which we would propound to-day,
yet God owned their word, and multitudes were saved.   And
if it were not perhaps too much like boasting of one's own
work under God, I might say, personally I have never found
the preaching of these doctrines lull this Church to sleep, but

ever while they have loved to maintain these truths, they have agonized for the souls of men, and the 1,600 or more whom I have myself baptized, upon profession of their faith, are living testimonies that these old truths in modern times have not lost their power to promote a revival of religion."[1]

In accounting for powerless preachers whose sermons affect no one, Spurgeon said: "The reason is, I believe, they do not know what *the gospel* is; they are afraid of *real gospel Calvinism*, and therefore the Lord does not own them."[2] In speaking of the influence of these doctrines on his own church he wrote: "Among the many candidates for baptism and church-membership who came forward every month, there were great numbers of young people, and others of riper years . . . I was delighted to hear them, one after another, not only express themselves clearly upon the great fundamental truth of justification by faith, but also give clear evidence that they were well instructed in the doctrines that cluster around the covenant of grace. I believe that one reason why our church has been, for these many years, so signally blessed of God, is that

---

[1] *The New Park Street and Metropolitan Tabernacle Pulpit*, Vol. VII, pp. 302-3.
The 1859 revival was itself an illustration of the connexion between Calvinistic doctrine and revivals. Other leaders in the awakening, such as Brownlow North (whose preaching was so widely influential in Scotland and Ireland), recognized this: "It is not unworthy of being noted that the vast majority of those servants of God who have been honoured by Him in producing revivals on a national scale, from the English Wycliffe and Bohemian Huss to those of the present, have been Augustinian or Calvinistic in their theological views . . . Brownlow North's teaching was in all points most pronouncedly Calvinistic. Indeed, so much was this the case that it seems marvellous that it obtained such very wide popularity." (*Records and Recollections of Brownlow North* (1810-75), by K. Moody-Stuart, p. 258.)
Andrew Bonar in his Preface to the second edition of *The Memoirs of Dr. Nettleton* (1783-1844), published in 1860, wrote: "Ireland, Wales and Scotland have been, during the past year, the theatre of the Spirit's mighty works, in a way not inferior to what was witnessed in the time of Nettleton. And let us not fail to note that the very same Calvinism which was wielded so effectually by Dr. Nettleton in his day, amid the scenes of revival wherein he was used as an instrument, has been used in our day, and in our land, by the great head of the Church . . . Who can say that Calvinistic doctrine has clogged the wheels of the chariot, when he casts his eye over the churches in Ireland, Wales and Scotland, where these have been the truths believed and proclaimed, while the Holy Spirit has come down in power and majesty?"
[2] *C. H. Spurgeon's Autobiography*, Vol. II, p. 99.

the great majority of those who have been added to our ranks have been well established in the old-fashioned faith of the Puritans and the Covenanters, and therefore have not been turned aside or drawn away from us."[1] "Brethren," Spurgeon exhorted his fellow ministers, " in proportion as a ministry is truthful, other things being equal, God can bless it. Would you have the Holy Ghost set His seal to a lie? Would you have Him bless what He has not revealed, and confirm with signs following that which is not truth? I am more and more persuaded that, if we mean to have God with us, we must keep to the truth."[2]

Error concerning the above doctrines Spurgeon regarded as undermining the very Gospel itself. Arminianism—the error that Christ died for the salvation of all and that man must decide for Christ before God can convert him—he openly condemned: " What is the heresy of Rome, but the addition of something to the perfect merits of Jesus Christ—the bringing in of the works of the flesh, to assist in our justification? And what is the heresy of Arminianism but the addition of something to the work of the Redeemer? . . . I have my own private opinion that there is no such thing as preaching Christ and Him crucified, unless we preach what nowadays is called Calvinism. It is a nickname to call it Calvinism; Calvinism is the gospel, and nothing else. I do not believe we can preach the gospel, if we do not preach justification by faith, without works; nor unless we preach the sovereignty of God in His dispensation of grace; nor unless we exalt the electing, unchangeable, eternal, immutable, conquering love of Jehovah; nor do I think we can preach the gospel unless we base it upon the special and particular redemption of His elect and chosen people which Christ wrought out upon the cross; nor can I comprehend a gospel which lets saints fall away after they are called. Such a gospel I abhor."[3]

About the year 1859 Spurgeon preached in Brighton. Not long after, Brighton newspapers announced that he had given up his Calvinistic doctrines, whereupon Spurgeon sent the

---

[1] *Ibid.,* Vol. II, p. 225.
[2] *An All-Round Ministry,* Addresses by C. H. Spurgeon, p. 350.
[3] *Autobiography,* Vol. I, p. 172.

following lines to the *Brighton Examiner*: "The statement you have made with regard to my recantation of Calvinistic doctrine is a fabrication from beginning to end, and one which could only have been invented for malicious purposes. I am the same in doctrine as I have ever been, and I hope to remain faithful to the same grand truth until death."[1] After revising his early sermons for republication many years later, Spurgeon wrote: "I was happy to find that I had no occasion to alter any of the doctrines which I preached in those early days of my ministry . . . as to the truths themselves, I stand just where I did when the Lord first revealed them to me."[2]

Spurgeon died in 1892. He lived long enough to see around him a terrible decline from sound doctrine. Towards the end he was regarded as "the last of the Puritans," and seemed almost to stand alone for the truth.[3] "We feel," he declared, "that a hardening process is going on among the masses . . . Things are not now as in our early ministry . . . Why is this? Whence this distaste for the ordinary services of the sanctuary? I believe that the answer, in some measure, lies in a direction little suspected. There has been a growing pandering to sensationalism . . . I would condemn no one, but I confess that I feel deeply grieved at some of the inventions of modern mission work."[4]

In 1892 the tide of popular thought in the churches was very different from what it had been in 1859, and the theology of 1892 became, as Spurgeon prophesied, the theology of the first half of the twentieth century: "What is being done to-day will affect the next centuries . . . For my part, I am quite willing to be eaten of dogs for the next fifty years; but the more distant future shall vindicate me."[5] Now a hundred years have passed since the last great national revival. Surely the time has come for us to reconsider the fruits of the theo-

---

[1] *The Life and Work of C. H. Spurgeon*, by G. Holden Pike, Vol. II, p. 327.
[2] *Autobiography*, Vol. II, p. 158.
[3] *Mr. Spurgeon stands alone among the modern leaders of Evangelical Nonconformists in his fidelity to the older Calvinistic creed.* R. W. Dale, 1881. Cf. *The Sword and Trowel*, 1881, p. 85.
[4] *An All-Round Ministry*, pp. 304-6.
[5] *An All-Round Ministry*, p. 368.

2

logical changes which have taken place since then. Have these changes really contributed to promoting more frequent revivals? To increasing the power of godliness? To convicting the world of sin? To filling churches with anxious hearers? Let us, as we read these sermons, face the obvious fact—a great change has taken place—is it for better or for worse? Is the church empowered or impoverished by modern views of the gospel and of evangelism? If Spurgeon's was true Gospel preaching, then in how many places is the pure Gospel preached with power to-day? May the centenary of the 1859 Revival cause many to consider such questions and to seek such an awakening as was witnessed in our land a hundred years ago.

THE PUBLISHERS.

March, 1959.

The Story of God's Mighty Acts[1]

"We have heard with our ears, O God, our fathers have told us, what work thou didst in their days, in the times of old."—Psalm xliv. 1.

PERHAPS there are no stories that stick by us so long as those which we hear in our childhood, those tales which are told us by our fathers, and in our nurseries. It is a sad reflection that too many of these stories are idle and vain, so that our minds in early infancy are tinctured with fables, and inoculated with strange and lying narratives. Now, among the early Christians and the old believers in the far-off times, nursery tales were far different from what they are now, and the stories with which their children were amused were of a far different class from those which fascinated us in the days of our babyhood. No doubt, Abraham would talk to young children about the flood, and tell them how the waters overspread the earth, and how Noah alone was saved in the ark. The ancient Israelites, when they dwelt in their own land, would all of them tell their children about the Red Sea, and the plagues which God wrought in Egypt when he brought his people out of the house of bondage. Among the early Christians we know that it was the custom of parents to recount to their children everything concerning the life of Christ, the acts of the apostles and the like interesting narratives. Nay, among our puritanic ancestors such were the stories that regaled their childhood. Sitting down by the fireside, before those old Dutch tiles with the quaint eccentric drawings upon them of the history of Christ, mothers would teach their children about Jesus walking on the water, or of his multiplying the loaves of bread, or of his marvellous transfiguration, or of the crucifixion of Jesus. Oh how I would that the like were the tales of the present age, that the stories of our childhood would be again the stories of Christ, and that we would each of us believe that, after all, there can be nothing so interesting as that which is true, and

[1] Sunday morning, July 17th, 1859.

19

nothing more striking than those stories which are written in sacred writ; nothing that can more truly move the heart of a child than the marvellous works of God which he did in the olden times. Now, it seems that the psalmist who wrote this most musical ode had heard from his father, handed to him by tradition, the stories of the wondrous things which God had done in his day; and afterwards, this sweet singer in Israel taught it to his children, and so was one generation after another led to call God blessed, remembering his mighty acts.

Now, my dear friends, this morning I intend to recall to your minds some of the wondrous things which God has done in the olden time. My aim and object will be to excite your minds to seek after the like, that looking back upon what God has done, you may be induced to look forward with the eye of expectation, hoping that he will again stretch forth his potent hand and his holy arm, and repeat those mighty acts he performed in ancient days.

First, I shall speak of *the marvellous stories which our fathers have told us, and which we have heard of the olden time;* secondly, I shall mention *some disadvantages under which these old stories labour with regard to the effect upon our minds;* and, then, I shall *draw the proper inferences from those marvellous things which we have heard that the Lord did in days of yore.*

I. To begin then, with THE WONDERFUL STORIES WE HAVE HEARD OF THE LORD'S ANCIENT DOINGS.

We have heard that God has at times done very mighty acts. The plain every-day course of the world hath been disturbed with wonders at which men have been exceedingly amazed. God hath not always permitted his church to go on climbing by slow degrees to victory, but he hath been pleased at times to smite one terrible blow, and lay his enemies down upon the earth, and bid his children march over their prostrate bodies. Turn ye back then, to ancient records, and remember what God hath done. Will ye not remember what he did at the Red Sea, how he smote Egypt and all its chivalry, and covered Pharaoh's chariot and horse in the Red Sea? Have ye not heard tell how God smote Og, king of Bashan, and Sihon, king of the Amorites, because they withstood the progress of his people? Have ye not learned how he proved that his mercy endureth for ever, when he slew those great kings and cast the mighty ones down from their thrones? Have you not read, too, how God smote the children of Canaan, and drove out the inhabitants thereof, and gave the land to his people, to be a possession by lot for ever? Have you not heard how when the hosts of Jabin came against them, the stars in their courses fought against Sisera? The river of Kishon swept them away, "that ancient river, the river Kishon," and there was none of them left? Hath it not been told you, too, how by the hand of David, God smote the Philistines, and how by his right hand he smote the children of Ammon? Have you not heard how Midian was put to confusion, and the myriads of Arabia were scattered by Asa in the day of his faith? And have ye not heard, too, how the Lord sent a blast upon the hosts of Sennacherib, so that in the morning they were all dead men? Tell —tell ye these, his wonders! Speak of them in your streets. Teach them to your children. Let them not be forgotten, for the right hand of the Lord hath done marvellous things, his name is known in all the earth.

The wonders, however, which most concern us, are those of the Christian era; and surely these are not second to those under the Old Testament. Have you never read how God won to himself great renown on the day of Pentecost? Turn ye to this book of the record of the wonders of the Lord and read. Peter the fisherman stood up and preached in the name of the Lord his God. A multitude assembled and the Spirit of God fell upon them; and it came to pass that three thousand in one day were pricked in their heart by the hand of God, and believed on the Lord Jesus Christ. And know you not how the twelve apostles with the disciples went everywhere preaching the Word, and the idols fell from their thrones. The cities opened wide their gates, and the messenger of Christ walked through the street and preached. It is true that at first they were driven hither and thither, and hunted like partridges upon the mountains; but do ye not remember how the Lord did get unto himself a victory, so that in a hundred years after the nailing of Christ to the cross, the gospel had been preached in every nation, and the isles of the sea had heard the sound thereof? And have ye yet forgotten how the heathen were baptized, thousands at a time, in every river? What stream is there in Europe that cannot testify to the majesty of the gospel? What city is there in the land that cannot tell how God's truth has triumphed, and how the heathen has forsaken his false gods, and bowed his knee to Jesus the crucified? The first spread of the gospel is a miracle never to be eclipsed. Whatever God may have done at the Red Sea, he hath done still more within a hundred years after the time when Christ first came into the world. It seemed as if a fire from heaven ran along the ground. Nothing could resist its force. The lightning shaft of truth shivered every pinnacle of the idol temple, and Jesus was worshipped from the rising of the sun to the going down of the same.

This is one of the things we have heard of the olden times.

And have ye never heard of the mighty things which God did by preachers some hundreds of years from that date? Hath it not been told you concerning Chrysostom, the golden-mouthed, how, whenever he preached, the church was thronged with attentive hearers; and there, standing and lifting up holy hands, he spake with a majesty unparalleled, the word of God in truth and righteousness; the people listening, hanging forward to catch every word, and anon breaking the silence with the clapping of their hands and the stamping of their feet; then silent again for awhile, spell-bound by the mighty orator; and anon carried away with enthusiasm, springing to their feet, clapping their hands, and shouting for joy again? Numberless were the conversions in his day, God was exceedingly magnified, for sinners were abundantly saved. And have your fathers never told you of the wondrous things that were done afterwards when the black darkness of superstition covered the earth, when Popery sat upon her ebon throne and stretched her iron rod across the nations and shut the windows of heaven, and quenched the very stars of God and made thick darkness cover the people? Have ye never heard how Martin Luther arose and preached the gospel of the grace of God, and how the nations trembled, and the world heard the voice of God and lived? Have ye not heard of Zwingle among the Swiss, and of Calvin in the holy city of Geneva, and of the mighty works that God did by them? Nay, as Britons have ye forgotten the mighty preacher of the truth —have your ears ceased to tingle with the wondrous tale of the preachers that Wickliffe sent forth into every market town and every hamlet of England, preaching the gospel of God? Oh, doth not history tell us that these men were like firebrands in the midst of the dry stubble; that their voice was as the roaring of a lion, and their going forth like the springing of a young lion. Their glory was as the firstling of a bullock; they did push the nation before them, and as for the enemies, they said, "Destroy them." None could stand before them, for the Lord their God had girded them with might.

To come down a little nearer to our own times, truly our fathers have told us the wondrous things which God did in the days of Wesley and of Whitefield. The churches were all asleep. Irreligion was the rule of the day. The very streets seemed to run with iniquity, and the gutters were filled full with the iniquity of sin. Up rose Whitefield and Wesley, men whose hearts the Lord had touched, and they dared to preach the gospel of the grace of God. Suddenly, as in a moment, there was heard the rush as of wings, and the church said: "Who are these that fly as a cloud, and as the doves to their windows?" They come! they come! numberless as the birds of heaven, with a rushing, like mighty winds that are not to be withstood. Within a few years, from the preaching of these two men, England was permeated with evangelical truth. The Word of God was known in every town, and there was scarcely a hamlet into which the Methodists had not penetrated. In those days of the slow-coach, when Christianity seemed to have bought up the old waggons in which our fathers once travelled —where business runs with steam, there oftentimes religion creeps along with its belly on the earth—we are astonished at these tales, and we think them wonders. Yet let us believe them; they come to us as substantial matters of history. And the wondrous things which God did in the olden times, by his grace he will yet do again. He that is mighty hath done great things and holy is his name.

There is a special feature to which I would call your attention with regard to the works of God in the olden time; they derive increasing interest and wonder from the fact that they were all sudden things. The old-stagers in our churches believe that things must grow, gently, by degrees; we must go step by step onward. Concentrated action and continued labour, they say, will ultimately bring success. But the marvel is, all God's works have been sudden. When Peter stood up to preach, it did not take six weeks to convert the three thousand. They were converted at once and baptized that very day; they were that hour turned to God, and became as truly disciples of Christ as they could have been if their conversion had taken seventy years. So was it in the day of Martin Luther: it did not take Luther centuries to break through the thick darkness of Rome. God lit the candle and the candle burned, and there was the light in an instant—God works suddenly. If any one could have stood in Wurtemburg, and have said: "Can Popery be made to quail, can the Vatican be made to shake?" the answer would have been: "No; it will take at least a thousand years to do it. Popery, the great serpent, hath so twisted itself about the nations, and bound them so fast in its coil, that they cannot be delivered except by a long process." "Not so," however, did God say. He smote the dragon sorely, and the nations went free; he cut the gates of brass, and broke in sunder the bars of iron, and the people were delivered in an hour. Freedom came not in the course of years, but in an instant. The people that walked in darkness saw a great light, and upon them that dwelt in the land of the shadow of death, did the light shine. So was it in Whitefield's day. The rebuking of a slumbering church was not the work of ages; it was done at once. Have ye never heard of the great revival under Whitefield? Take as an instance that at Cambuslang. He was preaching in the churchyard to a great congregation, that could not get into any edifice; and while preaching, the power of God came upon the people, and one after another fell down as if they were smitten; and it was estimated that not less than three thousand persons were crying out at one time under the conviction of sin. He preached on, now thundering like Boanerges, and then comforting like Barnabas, and the work spread, and no tongue can tell the great things that God did under that one sermon of Whitefield. Not even the sermon of Peter on the day of Pentecost was equal to it.

So has it been in all revivals; God's work has been done suddenly. As with a clap of thunder has God descended from on high; not slowly, but on cherubim right royally doth he ride;

on the wings of the mighty wind does he fly. Sudden has been the work; men could scarce believe it true, it was done in so short a space of time. Witness the great revival which is going on in and around Belfast. After carefully looking at the matter, and after seeing a trusty and well-beloved brother who lived in that neighbourhood, I am convinced, notwithstanding what enemies may say, that it is a genuine work of grace, and that God is doing wonders there. A friend who called to see me yesterday, tells me that the lowest and vilest men, the most depraved females in Belfast, have been visited with this extraordinary epilepsy, as the world calls it; but with this strange rushing of the Spirit, as we have it. Men who have been drunkards have suddenly felt an impulse compelling them to pray. They have resisted; they have sought to their cups in order to put it out; but when they have been swearing, seeking to quench the Spirit by their blasphemy, God has at last brought them on their knees, and they have been compelled to cry for mercy with piercing shrieks, and to agonize in prayer; and then after a time, the Evil one seems to have been cast out of them, and in a quiet, holy, happy frame of mind, they have made a profession of their faith in Christ, and have walked in his fear and love. Roman Catholics have been converted. I thought that an extraordinary thing; but they have been converted very frequently indeed in Ballymena and in Belfast. In fact, I am told the priests are now selling small bottles of holy water for people to take, in order that they may be preserved from this desperate contagion of the Holy Spirit. This holy water is said to have such efficacy, that those who do not attend any of the meetings are not likely to be meddled with by the Holy Spirit—so the priests tell them. But if they go to the meetings, even this holy water cannot preserve them—they are as liable to fall a prey to the Divine influence. I think they are just as likely to do so without as with it. All this has been brought about suddenly, and although we may expect to find some portion of *natural* excitement, yet I am persuaded it is in the main a real, *spiritual*, and an abiding work. There is a little froth on the surface, but there is a deep running current that is not to be resisted, sweeping underneath, and carrying everything before it. At least, there is something to awaken our interest, when we understand that in the small town of

Ballymena on market day, the publicans have always taken one hundred pounds for whiskey, and now they cannot take a sovereign all day long in all the public houses. Men who were once drunkards now meet for prayer, and people after hearing one sermon will not go until the minister has preached another, and sometimes a third; and at last he is obliged to say: "You must go, I am exhausted." Then they will break up into groups in their streets and in their houses, crying out to God to let this mighty work spread, that sinners may be converted unto him. "Well," says one, "we cannot believe it." Very likely you cannot, but some of us can, for we have heard it with our ears, and our fathers have told us the mighty works that God did in their days, and we are prepared to believe that God can do the like works now.

I must here remark that, in all these old stories, there is one very plain feature. Whenever God has done a mighty work it has been by some very insignificant instrument. When he slew Goliath it was by little David, who was but a ruddy youth. Lay not up the sword of Goliath—I always thought that a mistake of David—lay up, not Goliath's sword, but lay up the stone and treasure up the sling in God's armoury for ever. When God would slay Sisera, it was a woman that must do it with a hammer and a nail. God has done his mightiest works by the meanest instruments: that is a fact most true of all God's works. Peter the fisherman at Pentecost, Luther the humble monk at the Reformation, Whitefield the potboy of the Old Bell Inn at Gloucester in the time of the last century's revival; and so it must be to the end. God works not by Pharaoh's horses or chariot, but he works by Moses' rod; he doth not his wonders with the whirlwind and the storm; he doth them by the still small voice, that the glory may be his and the honour all his own. Doth not this open a field of encouragement to you and to me? Why may not we be employed in doing some mighty work for God here? Moreover, we have noticed in all these stories of God's mighty works in the olden time, that wherever he has done any great thing it has been by someone who has had very great faith. I do verily believe at this moment that, if God willed it, every soul in this hall would be converted now. If God chose to put forth the operations of his own mighty Spirit, not the most obdurate heart would be able to stand against it. "He will have mercy upon whom he will have mercy." He will do as he pleases; none can stay his hand. "Well," says one, "but I do not expect to see any great things." Then, my dear friend, you will not be disappointed, for you will not see them; but those that expect them *shall* see them. Men of great faith do great things. It was Elijah's faith that slew the priests of Baal. If he had had the little heart that some of you have, Baal's priests had still ruled over the people, and would never have been smitten with the sword. It was Elijah's faith that bade him say: "If the Lord be God, follow him, but if Baal, then follow him." And again: "Choose one bullock for yourselves, cut it in pieces, lay it on wood and put no fire under, call ye on the name of your gods, and I will call on the name of Jehovah." It was his noble faith that bade him say: "Take the prophets of Baal; let not one of them escape"; and he brought them down to the brook Kishon, and slew them there—a holocaust to God. The reason why God's name was so magnified, was because Elijah's faith in God was so mighty and heroic. When the Pope sent his bull to Luther, Luther burned it. Standing up in the midst of the crowd with the blazing paper in his hand he said: "See here, this is the Pope's bull." What cared he for all the Popes that were ever in or out of hell? And when he went to Worms to meet the grand Diet, his followers said: "You are in danger, stand back." "No," said Luther, "if there were as many devils in Worms as there are tiles on the roofs of the houses, I would not fear; I will go"—and into Worms he went, confident in the Lord his God. It was the same with Whitefield; he believed and he expected that God would do great things. When he went into his pulpit he believed that God would bless the people, and God did do so. Little faith may do little things, but great faith shall be greatly honoured. O God! our fathers have told us this, that whenever they had great faith thou hast always honoured it by doing mighty works.

I will detain you no longer on this point, except to make one observation. All the mighty works of God, have been attended with great prayer, as well as with great faith. Have ye ever heard of the commencement of the great American revival? A man unknown and obscure, laid it up in his heart to pray that God would bless his country. After praying and wrestling and making the soul-stirring enquiry: "Lord, what wilt thou have *me* to do? Lord, what wilt thou have me *to do*?" he hired a room, and put up an announcement that there would be a prayer-meeting held there at such-and-such an hour of the day. He went at the proper hour, and there was not a single person there; he began to pray, and prayed for half an hour alone. One came in at the end of the half-hour, and then two more, and I think he closed with six. The next week came round, and there might have been fifty dropped in at different times; at last the prayer-meeting grew to a hundred, then others began to start prayer-meetings; at last there was scarcely a street in New York that was without a prayer-meeting. Merchants found time to run in, in the middle of the day, to pray. The prayer-meetings became daily ones, lasting for about an hour; petitions and requests were sent up, these were simply asked and offered before God, and the answers came; and many were the happy hearts that stood up and testified that the prayer offered last week had been already fulfilled. Then it was when they were all earnest in prayer, suddenly the Spirit of God fell upon the people, and it was rumoured that in a certain village a preacher had been preaching in thorough earnest, and there had been hundreds converted in a week. The matter spread into and through the Northern States—these revivals of religion became universal, and it has been sometimes said that a quarter of a million of people were converted to God through the short space of two or three months. Now the same effect was produced in Ballymena and Belfast by the same means. The brother thought that it lay at his heart to pray, and he did pray; then he held a regular prayer-meeting; day after day they met together to entreat the blessing, and the fire descended and the work was done. Sinners were converted, not by ones or twos, but by hundreds and thousands, and the Lord's name was greatly magnified by the progress of his gospel. Beloved, I am only telling you *facts*. Make each of you your own estimate of them if you please.

II. Agreeably to my division, I have now to make a few observations upon the DISADVANTAGES UNDER WHICH THESE OLD STORIES FREQUENTLY LABOUR. When people hear about what God used to do, one of the things they say is: "Oh, that was a very long while ago." They imagine that times have altered since then. Says one: "I can believe anything about the Reformation—the largest accounts that can possibly be given, I can take in." "And so could I concerning Whitefield and Wesley," says another, "all that is quite true, they did labour vigorously and successfully, but that was many years ago. Things were in a different state then from what they are now." Granted; but I want to know what the things have to do with it. I thought it was God that did it. Has God changed? Is he not an immutable God, the same yesterday, to-day and for ever? Does not that furnish an argument to prove that what God has done at one time he can do at another? Nay, I think I may push it a little further, and say what he has done once, is a prophecy of what he intends to do again—that the mighty works which have been accomplished in the olden time shall all be repeated, and the Lord's song shall be sung again in Zion, and he shall again be greatly glorified. Others among you say, "Oh, well I look upon these things as great prodigies —miracles. We are not to expect them every day." That is the very reason why we do not get them. If we had learnt to expect them, we should no doubt obtain them, but we put them up on the shelf, as being out of the common order of our moderate religion, as being mere curiosities of Scripture history. We imagine such things, however true, to be prodigies of providence; we cannot imagine them to be according to the ordinary working of his mighty power. I beseech you, my friends, abjure that idea, put it out of your mind. Whatever God has done in the way of converting sinners is to be looked upon as a precedent, for "his arm is not shortened that he cannot save, nor is his ear heavy that he cannot hear." If we are straitened at all, we are not straitened in him, we are straitened in our own bowels. Let us take the blame of it ourselves, and with earnestness seek that God would restore to us the faith of the men of old, that we may richly enjoy his grace as in the days of old. Yet there is another disadvantage under which these old stories labour. The fact is, we have not seen them. Why, I may talk to you ever so long about revivals, but you won't believe them half so much, nor half so truly, as if one were to occur in your very midst. If you saw it with your own eyes, then you would see the power of it. If you had

lived in Whitefield's day, or had heard Grimshaw preach, you
would believe anything. Grimshaw would preach twenty-
four times a week: he would preach many times in the course
of a sultry day, going from place to place on horseback. That
man *did* preach. It seemed as if heaven would come down to
earth to listen to him. He spoke with a real earnestness, with
all the fire of zeal that ever burned in mortal breast, and the
people trembled while they listened to him, and said, "Certainly this is the voice of God." It was the same with Whitefield. The people would seem to move to and fro while he
spoke, even as the harvest field is moved with the wind. So
mighty was the energy of God that after hearing such a sermon
the hardest-hearted men would go away and say: "There
must be something in it, I never heard the like." Can you not
realise these as literal facts? Do they stand up in all their
brightness before your eyes? Then I think the stories you
have heard with your ears should have a true and proper effect
upon your own lives.

III. This brings me in the third place to the PROPER IN-
FERENCES THAT ARE TO BE DRAWN FROM THE OLD STORIES OF
GOD'S MIGHTY DEEDS.

I would that I could speak with the fire of some of those men
whose names I have mentioned. Pray for me, that the Spirit
of God may rest upon me, that I may plead with you for a little
time with all my might, seeking to exhort and stir you up, that
you may get a like revival in your midst. My dear friends, the
first effect which the reading of the history of God's mighty
works should have upon us, is that of gratitude and praise.
Have we nothing to sing about to-day?—then let us sing concerning days of yore. If we cannot sing to our well-beloved a
song concerning what he is doing in our midst, let us, nevertheless, take down our harps from the willows, and sing an old
song, and bless and praise his holy name for the things which
he did to his ancient church, for the wonders which he wrought
in Egypt, and in all the lands wherein he led his people, and
from which he brought them out with a high hand and with
an outstretched arm. When we have thus begun to praise God
for what he has done, I think I may venture to impress upon
you one other great day. Let what God has done suggest to
you the prayer that he would repeat the like signs and won-

ders among us. Oh! men and brethren, what would this heart feel if I could but believe that there were some among you who would go home and pray for a revival of religion—men whose faith is large enough, and their love fiery enough to lead them from this moment to exercise unceasing intercessions that God would appear among us and do wondrous things here, as in the times of former generations. Why, look you here in this present assembly what objects there are for our compassion. Glancing round, I observe one and another whose history I may happen to know, but how many are there still unconverted—men who have trembled and who know they have, but have shaken off their fears, and once more are daring their destiny, determined to be suicides to their own souls and to put away from them that grace which once seemed as if it were striving in their hearts. They are turning away from the gates of heaven, and running post-haste to the doors of hell; and will not you stretch out your hands to God to stop them in this desperate resolve? If in this congregation there were but one unconverted man and I could point him out and say: "There he sits, one soul that has never felt the love of God, and never has been moved to repentance," with what anxious curiosity would every eye regard him. I think out of the thousands of Christians here, there is not one who would refuse to go home and pray for that solitary, unconverted individual. But, oh! my brethren, it is not one that is in danger of hell fire; here are hundreds and thousands of our fellow-creatures.

Shall I give you yet another reason why you should pray? Hitherto all other means have been used without effect. God is my witness how often I have striven in this pulpit to be the means of the conversion of men. I have preached my very heart out. I could say no more than I have said, and I hope the secrecy of my chamber is a witness to the fact that I do not cease to feel when I cease to speak; but I have a heart to pray for those of you who are never affected, or who, if affected, still quench the Spirit of God. My hearers, I have done my utmost. Will not you come to the help of the Lord against the mighty? Will not your prayers accomplish that which my preaching fails to do? Here they are; I commend them to you: men and women whose hearts refuse to melt, whose stubborn knees will not bend; I give them up to you and ask you to pray for them. Carry their cases on your knees before God. Wife! never cease to pray for your unconverted husband. Husband! never stay your supplication till you see your wife converted. And, O fathers and mothers! have you no unconverted children? Have you not brought them here many and many a Sunday, and they remain just as they have been? You have sent them first to one chapel and then to another, and they are just what they were. The wrath of God abideth on them. Die they must; and should they die now, to a certainty you are aware that the flames of hell must engulf them. And do you refuse to pray for them? Hard hearts, brutish souls, if knowing Christ yourself ye will not pray for those who come of your own loins—your children according to the flesh.

Dear friends, we do not know what God may do for us if we do but pray for a blessing. Look at the movement we have already seen; we have witnessed Exeter Hall, St. Paul's Cathedral and Westminster Abbey crammed to the doors, but we have seen no effect as yet of all these mighty gatherings. Have we not tried to preach without trying to pray? Is it not likely that the church has been putting forth its preaching hand but not its praying hand? O dear friends! let us agonize in prayer, and it shall come to pass that this Music Hall shall witness the sighs and groans of the penitent and the songs of the converted. It shall yet happen that this vast host shall not come and go as now it does, but little the better; but men shall go out of this hall, praising God and saying: "It was good to be there; it was none other than the house of God, and the very gate of heaven." Thus much to stir you up to prayer.

Another inference we should draw is that all the stories we have heard should correct any self-dependence which may have crept into our treacherous hearts. Perhaps we as a congregation have begun to depend upon our numbers and so forth. We may have thought: "Surely God must bless us through the ministry." Now let the stories which our fathers have told us remind you, and remind me, that God saves not by many nor by few; that it is not in us to do this but God must do it all; it may be that some hidden preacher, whose name has never been known, some obscure denizen of St. Giles, will yet start up in this city of London and preach the

Lord with greater power than bishops or ministers have ever known before. I will welcome him; God be with him, let him come from where he may, only let God speed him, and let the work be done. Mayhap, however, God intends to bless the agency used in this place for your good and for your conversion. If so, I am thrice happy to think such should be the case. But place no dependence upon the instrument. No, when men laughed at us and mocked us most, God blessed us most; and now it is not a disreputable thing to attend the Music Hall. We are not so much despised as we once were, but I question whether we have so great a blessing as once we had. We would be willing to endure another pelting in the pillory, to go through another ordeal with every newspaper against us, and with every man hissing and abusing us, if God so pleases, if he will but give us a blessing. But let him cast out of us any idea that our own bow and our own sword will get us the victory. We shall never get a revival here unless we believe that it is the Lord, and the Lord alone, that can do it.

Having made this statement, I will endeavour to stir you up with confidence that the result that I have pictured may be obtained, and that the stories we have heard of the olden times may become true in our day. Why should not every one of my hearers be converted? Is there any limitation in the Spirit of God? Why should not the feeblest minister become the means of salvation to thousands? Is God's arm shortened? My brethren, when I bid you pray that God would make the ministry quick and powerful, like a two-edged sword, for the salvation of sinners, I am not setting you a hard, much less an impossible, task. We have but to ask and to get. Before we call, God will answer; and while we are yet speaking he will hear. God alone can know what may come of this morning's sermon, if he chooses to bless it. From this moment you may pray more; from this moment God may bless the ministry more. From this hour other pulpits may become more full of life and vigour than before. From this same moment the Word of God may flow, and run, and rush, and get to itself an amazing and boundless victory. Only wrestle in prayer, meet together in your houses, go to your private room, be instant, be earnest in season and out of season, agonize for souls, and all that you have heard shall be forgotten in what ye shall see;

and all that others have told you shall be as nothing compared with what ye shall hear with your ears and behold with your eyes in your own midst.   Oh ye, to whom all this is as an idle tale, who love not God, neither serve him, I beseech you stop and think for a moment.   Oh, Spirit of God, rest on thy servant while a few sentences are uttered, and make them mighty. God has striven with some of you.   You have had your times of conviction.   You are trying now, perhaps, to be infidels. You are trying to say now: "There is no hell—there is no hereafter."   It will not do.   You know there is a hell and all the laughter of those who seek to ruin your souls cannot make you believe that there is not.   You sometimes try to think so, but you know that God is true.   I do not argue with you now. Conscience tells you that God will punish you for sin.   Depend upon it you will find no happiness in trying to stifle God's Spirit.   This is not the path to bliss, to quench those thoughts which would lead you to Christ.   I beseech you, take off your hands from God's arm; resist not still his Spirit.   Bow the knee and lay hold of Christ and believe on him.   It will come to this yet.   God the Holy Spirit will have you.   I do trust that in answer to many prayers he intends to save you yet.   Give way now, but oh, remember if you are successful in quenching the Spirit, your success will be the most awful disaster that can ever occur to you, for if the Spirit forsake you, you are lost.   It may be that this is the last warning you will ever have.   The conviction you are now trying to put down and stifle may be the last you will ever have, and the angel standing with the black seal and the wax may be now about to drop it upon your destiny, and say: "Let him alone.   He chooses drunkenness—he chooses lust—let him have them; and let him reap the wages in the everlasting fires of hell." Sinners, believe on the Lord Jesus: repent and be converted, every one of you.   I am bold to say what Peter did.   Breaking through every bond of every kind that could bind my lip, I exhort you in God's name, repent and escape from damnation. A few more months and years, and ye shall know what damnation means, except ye repent.   Oh! fly to Christ while yet the lamp holds out and burns, and mercy is still preached to you. Grace is still presented; accept Christ, resist him no longer; come to him now.   The gates of mercy are wide open to-day;

come now, poor sinner, and have thy sins forgiven. When the old Romans used to attack a city, it was sometimes their custom to set up at the gate a white flag, and if the garrison surrendered while that white flag was there, their lives were spared. After that the black flag was put up, and then every man was put to the sword. The white flag is up to-day; perhaps to-morrow the black flag will be elevated upon the pole of the law and then there is no repentance or salvation either in this world or in that which is to come. An old eastern conqueror when he came to a city used to light a brazier of coals, and, setting it high upon a pole he would, with sound of trumpet, proclaim that if they surrendered while the lamp held out and burned he would have mercy upon them, but that when the coals were out he would storm the city, pull it stone from stone, sow it with salt, and put men and women and children to a bloody death. To-day the thunders of God bid you to take the like warning. There is your light, the lamp, the brazier of hot coals. Year after year the fire is dying out, nevertheless there is coal left. Even now the wind of death is trying to blow out the last live coal. Oh! sinner, turn while the lamp continues to blaze. Turn now, for when the last coal is dead thy repentance cannot avail thee. Thy everlasting yelling in torment cannot move the heart of God; thy groans and briny tears cannot move him to pity thee. To-day if ye will hear his voice, harden not your hearts as in the provocation. Oh, to-day lay hold on Christ: "Kiss the Son, lest he be angry, and ye perish from the way, when his wrath is kindled but a little. Blessed are all they that put their trust in him."

The Blood of the Everlasting Covenant[1]

"The blood of the everlasting covenant."—Hebrews xiii. 20.

ALL God's dealings with men have had a covenant character. It hath so pleased him to arrange it, that he will not deal with us except through a covenant, nor can we deal with him except in the same manner. Adam in the garden was under a covenant with God and God was in covenant with him. That covenant he speedily brake. There is a covenant still existing in all its terrible power—terrible I say, because it has been broken on man's part, and therefore God will most surely fulfil its solemn threatenings and sanctions. That is the covenant of works. By this he dealt with Moses, and in this doth he deal with the whole race of men as represented in the first Adam. Afterwards, when God would deal with Noah, it was by a covenant; and when in succeeding ages he dealt with Abraham, he was still pleased to bind himself to him by a covenant. That covenant he preserved and kept, and it was renewed continually to many of his seed. God dealt not even with David, the man after his own heart, except with a covenant. He made a covenant with his anointed; and beloved, he dealeth with you and me this day still by covenant. When he shall come in all his terrors to condemn, he shall smite by covenant— namely, by the sword of the covenant of Sinai; and if he comes in the splendours of his grace to save, he still comes to us by covenant—namely, the covenant of Zion; the covenant which he has made with the Lord Jesus Christ, the head and representative of his people. And mark, whenever we come into close and intimate dealings with God, it is sure to be, on our part, also by covenant. We make with God, after conversion, a covenant of gratitude; we come to him sensible of what he has done for us, and we devote ourselves to him. We set our seal to that covenant when in baptism we are united with his church; and day by day, so often as we come around the table of the breaking of bread, we renew the vow of our covenant,

[1] Sunday morning, October 2nd, 1859.

and thus we have personal intercourse with God. I cannot pray to him except through the covenant of grace; and I know that I am not his child unless I am his, first through the covenant whereby Christ purchased me, and secondly, through the covenant by which I have given up myself, and dedicated all that I am and all that I have to him. It is important, then, since the covenant is the only ladder which reaches from earth to heaven—since it is the only way in which God has intercourse with us, and by which we can deal with him, that we should know how to discriminate between covenant and covenant; and should not be in any darkness or error with regard to what is the covenant of grace, and what is not. It shall be my endeavour, this morning, to make as simple and as plain as possible, the matter of the covenant spoken of in our text, and I shall thus speak—firstly, upon the *covenant of grace*; secondly, *its everlasting character*; and thirdly, the relationship which the blood bears to it. " *The blood of the everlasting covenant.*"

I. First of all, then, I have to speak this morning of THE COVENANT mentioned in the text; and I observe that we can readily discover at first sight *what the covenant is not*. We see at once that this is not the covenant of works, for the simple reason that this is an everlasting covenant. Now the covenant of works was not everlasting in any sense whatever. It was not eternal; it was first made in the garden of Eden. It had a beginning, it has been broken; it will be violated continually, and will soon be wound up and pass away: therefore, it is not everlasting in any sense. The covenant of works cannot bear an everlasting title; but as the one in my text is an everlasting covenant, therefore it is not the covenant of works. God made a covenant first of all with the human race, which ran in this wise: " If thou, O man, wilt be obedient, thou shalt live and be happy, but if thou wilt be disobedient, thou shalt perish. In the day that thou disobeyest me thou shalt die." That covenant was made with all of us in the person of our representative, the first Adam. If Adam had kept that covenant, we believe we should every one of us have been preserved. But inasmuch as he broke the covenant, you and I, and all of us, fell down and were considered henceforth as the heirs of wrath, as inheritors of sin, as prone to every evil and subject to every misery. That covenant has passed away with regard to God's people; it has been put away through the new and better covenant which has utterly and entirely eclipsed it by its gracious glory.

Again, I may remark that the covenant here meant is not the covenant of gratitude which is made between the loving child of God and his Saviour. Such a covenant is very right and proper. I trust all of us who know the Saviour have said in our very hearts:

> " 'Tis done! the great transaction's done;
> I am my Lord's, and he is mine."

We have given up everything to him. But that covenant is not the one in the text, for the simple reason that the covenant in our text is an everlasting one. Now ours was only written out some few years ago. It would have been despised by us in the earlier parts of our life, and cannot at the very utmost be so old as ourselves.

Having thus readily shown what this covenant is not, I may observe *what this covenant is*. And here it will be necessary for me to subdivide this head again, and to speak of it thus: To understand a covenant, you must know who are the contracting parties; secondly, what are the stipulations of the contract; thirdly, what are the objects of it; and then, if you would go still deeper, you must understand something of the motives which lead the contracting parties to form the covenant between themselves.

1. Now, in this covenant of grace, we must first of all observe *the high contracting parties* between whom it was made. The covenant of grace was made before the foundation of the world between God the Father and God the Son; or to put it in a yet more scriptural light, it was made mutually between the three divine persons of the adorable Trinity. This covenant was not made directly between God and man. Man did not at that time exist; but Christ stood in the covenant as man's representative. In that sense we will allow that it was a covenant between God and man, but not a covenant between God and any man personally and individually. It was a covenant between God and Christ, and through Christ indirectly with all the blood-bought seed who were loved of

Christ from the foundation of the world.   It is a noble and glorious thought, the very poetry of that old Calvinistic doctrine which we teach, that long ere the day star knew its place, before God had spoken existence out of nothing, before angel's wing had stirred the unnavigated ether, before a solitary song had disturbed the solemnity of the silence in which God reigned supreme, he had entered into solemn counsel with himself, with his Son and with his Spirit, and had in that council decreed, determined, purposed and predestinated the salvation of his people.   He had, moreover, in the covenant arranged the ways and means, and fixed and settled everything which should work together for the effecting of the purpose and the decree.   My soul flies back now, winged by imagination and by faith, and looks into that mysterious council chamber, and by faith I behold the Father pledging himself to the Son, and the Son pledging himself to the Father, while the Spirit gives his pledge to both, and thus that divine compact, long to be hidden in darkness, is completed and settled—the covenant which in these latter days has been read in the light of heaven, and has become the joy and hope and boast of all the saints.

2. And now, what were *the stipulations of this covenant*? They were somewhat in this wise.   God had foreseen that man after creation would break the covenant of works; that however mild and gentle the tenure upon which Adam had possession of Paradise, yet that tenure would be too severe for him, and he would be sure to kick against it, and ruin himself. God had also foreseen that his elect ones, whom he had chosen out of the rest of mankind, would fall by the sin of Adam, since they, as well as the rest of mankind, were represented in Adam.   The covenant therefore had for its end the restoration of the chosen people.   And now we may readily understand what were the stipulations.   On the Father's part, thus runs the covenant.   I cannot tell you it in the glorious celestial tongue in which it was written: I am fain to bring it down to the speech which suiteth to the ear of flesh, and to the heart of a mortal.   Thus, I say, runs the covenant, in lines like these: " I, the Most High Jehovah, do hereby give unto my only begotten and well-beloved Son, a people, countless beyond the number of the stars, who shall be by him washed from sin, by

him preserved and kept and led, and by him, at last, presented before my throne, without spot or wrinkle or any such thing. I covenant by oath, and swear by myself, because I can swear by no greater, that these whom I now give to Christ shall be for ever the objects of my eternal love. Them will I forgive through the merit of the blood. To these will I give a perfect righteousness; these will I adopt and make my sons and daughters, and these shall reign with me through Christ eternally." Thus run that glorious side of the covenant. The Holy Spirit also, as one of the high contracting parties on this side of the covenant, gave his declaration: "I hereby covenant," saith he, "that all whom the Father giveth to the Son, I will in due time quicken. I will show them their need of redemption; I will cut off from them all groundless hope, and destroy their refuges of lies. I will bring them to the blood of sprinkling; I will give them faith whereby this blood shall be applied to them; I will work in them every grace; I will keep their faith alive; I will cleanse them and drive out all depravity from them, and they shall be presented at last spotless and faultless." This was the one side of the covenant, which is at this very day being fulfilled and scrupulously kept. As for the other side of the covenant this was the part of it, engaged and covenanted by Christ. He thus declared and covenanted with his Father: "My Father, on my part I covenant that in the fulness of time I will become man. I will take upon myself the form and nature of the fallen race. I will live in their wretched world, and for my people will I keep the law perfectly. I will work out a spotless righteousness, which shall be acceptable to the demands of thy just and holy law. In due time I will bear the sins of all my people. Thou shalt exact their debts on me; the chastisement of their peace I will endure, and by my stripes they shall be healed. My Father, I covenant and promise that I will be obedient unto death, even the death of the cross. I will magnify thy law and make it honourable. I will suffer all they ought to have suffered. I will endure the curse of thy law, and all the vials of thy wrath shall be emptied and spent upon my head. I will then rise again; I will ascend into heaven; I will intercede for them at thy right hand; and I will make myself responsible for every one of them, that not one of those whom

thou hast given me shall ever be lost, but I will bring all my
sheep of whom, by my blood, thou has constituted me the
shepherd—I will bring every one safe to thee at last." Thus
ran the covenant; and now, I think, you have a clear idea of
what it was and how it stands—the covenant between God and
Christ, between God the Father and God the Spirit, and God
the Son as the covenant head and representative of all God's
elect. I have told you, as briefly as I could, what were the
stipulations of it. You will please to remark, my dear friends,
that the covenant is, on one side, perfectly fulfilled. God the
Son has paid the debts of all the elect. He has, for us men and
for our redemption, suffered the whole of wrath divine. Nothing remaineth now on this side of the question except that he
shall continue to intercede, that he may safely bring all his
redeemed to glory.

On the side of the Father this part of the covenant has been
fulfilled to countless myriads. God the Father and God the
Spirit have not been behindhand in their divine contract.
And mark you, this side shall be as fully and as completely
finished and carried out as the other. Christ can say of what
he promised to do, "It is finished!" and the like shall be said
by all the glorious covenanters. All for whom Christ died
shall be pardoned, all justified, all adopted. The Spirit shall
quicken them all, shall give them all faith, shall bring them
all to heaven, and they shall, every one of them, without let or
hindrance, stand accepted in the beloved, in the day when the
people shall be numbered, and Jesus shall be glorified.

3. And now, having seen who were the high contracting
parties and what were the terms of the covenant made between them, let us see what were *the objects of this covenant*.
Was this covenant made for every man of the race of Adam?
Assuredly not; we discover the secret by the visible. That
which is in the covenant is to be seen in due time with the eye
and to be heard with the ear. I see multitudes of men perishing, continuing wantonly in their wicked ways, rejecting the
offer of Christ which is presented to them in the gospel day
after day, treading under foot the blood of the Son of Man,
defying the Spirit who strives with them; I see these men
going on from bad to worse and at last perishing in their sins.
I have not the folly to believe that they have any part in the

covenant of grace. Those who die impenitent, the multitudes who reject the Saviour, are clearly proved to have no part and no lot in the sacred covenant of divine grace; for if they were interested in that, there would be certain marks and evidences which would show us this. We should find that in due time in this life they would be brought to repentance, would be washed in the Saviour's blood, and would be saved. The covenant—to come at once straight to the matter, however offensive the doctrine may be—the covenant has relationship to the elect and none besides. Does this offend you? Be ye offended even more. What said Christ? " I pray for them: I pray not for the world, but for them which thou hast given me: for they are thine." If Christ prayeth for none but for his chosen, why should ye be angry that ye are also taught from the Word of God that in the covenant there was provision made for the like persons, that they might receive eternal life. As many as shall believe, as many as shall trust in Christ, as many as shall persevere unto the end, as many as shall enter into the eternal rest, so many and no more are interested in the covenant of divine grace.

4. Furthermore, we have to consider what were the motives of this covenant? Why was the covenant made at all? There was no compulsion or constraint on God. As yet there was no creature. Even could the creature have an influence on the Creator, there was none existing in the period when the covenant was made. We can look nowhere for God's motive in the covenant except it be in himself, for of God it could be said literally in that day: " I am, and there is none beside me." Why then did he make the covenant? I answer, absolute sovereignty dictated it. But why were certain men the objects of it and why not others? I answer, sovereign grace guided the pen. It was not the merit of man, it was nothing which God foresaw in us that made him choose many and leave others to go on in their sins. It was nothing in them, it was sovereignty and grace combined that made the divine choice. If you, my brethren and sisters, have a good hope that you are interested in the covenant of grace, you must sing that song—

" What was there in me to merit esteem, or give the Creator delight?
'Twas even so, Father, I ever must sing, for so it seemed good in thy sight."

" He will have mercy on whom he will have mercy," " for it is not of him that willeth, nor of him that runneth, but of God that showeth mercy." His sovereignty elected, and his grace distinguished, and immutability decreed. No motive dictated the election of the individuals, except a motive in himself of love and of divine sovereignty. Doubtless the grand intention of God in making the covenant at all was his own glory; any motive inferior to that would be beneath his dignity. God must find his motives in himself: he has not to look to moths and worms for motives for his deeds. He is the " I AM."

> " He sits on no precarious throne,
>   Nor borrows leave to be."

He doth as he wills in the armies of heaven. Who can stay his hand and say unto him, " What doest thou?" Shall the clay ask the potter for the motive for his making it into a vessel? Shall the thing formed before its creation dictate to its Creator? No, let God be God, and let man shrink into his native nothingness, and if God exalt him, let him not boast as though God found a reason for the deed in man. He finds his motives in himself. He is self-contained, and findeth nothing beyond nor needeth anything from any but himself. Thus have I, as fully as time permits this morning, discussed the first point concerning the covenant. May the Holy Spirit lead us into this sublime truth.

II. But now, in the second place, we come to notice ITS EVERLASTING CHARACTER. It is called an everlasting covenant. And here you observe at once its *antiquity*. The covenant of grace is the oldest of all things. It is sometimes a subject of great joy to me to think that the covenant of grace is older than the covenant of works. The covenant of works had a beginning, but the covenant of grace had not; and blessed be God the covenant of works has its end, but the covenant of grace shall stand fast when heaven and earth shall pass away. The antiquity of the covenant of grace demands our grateful attention. It is a truth which tends to elevate the mind. I know of no doctrine more grand than this. It is the very soul and essence of all poetry, and in sitting down and meditating upon it, I do confess my spirit has sometimes been ravished with delight. Can you conceive the idea that before all things

God thought of you? That when as yet he had not made his mountains, he had thought of thee, poor puny worm? Before the magnificent constellations began to shine, and ere the great centre of the world had been fixed, and all the mighty planets and divers worlds had been made to revolve around it, then had God fixed the centre of his covenant, and ordained the number of those lesser stars which should revolve round that blessed centre, and derive light therefrom. Why, when one is taken up with some grand conceptions of the boundless universe, when with the astronomers we fly through space, when we find it without end, and the starry hosts without number, does it not seem marvellous that God should give poor insignificant man the preference beyond even the whole universe besides? Oh this cannot make us proud, because it is a divine truth, but it must make us feel happy. Oh believer, you think yourself nothing, but God does not think so of you. Men despise you, but God remembered you before he made anything. The covenant of love which he made with his Son on your behalf is older than the hoary ages, and if ye fly back when as yet time had not begun, before those massive rocks that bear the marks of grey old age upon them had begun to be deposited, he had loved and chosen you, and made a covenant on your behalf. Remember well these ancient things of the eternal hills.

Then, again, it is an everlasting covenant from its *sureness*. Nothing is everlasting which is not secure. Man may erect his structures and think they may last for ever, but the Tower of Babel has crumbled, and the very Pyramids bear signs of ruin. Nothing which man has made is everlasting, because he cannot ensure it against decay. But as for the covenant of grace, well did David say of it: " It is ordered in all things and sure." It is—

> " Signed, and sealed, and ratified,
>   In all things ordered well."

There is not an " if " or a " but " in the whole of it from beginning to end. Freewill hates God's " shalls " and " wills," and likes man's " ifs " and " buts," but there are no " ifs " and " buts " in the covenant of grace. Thus the tenure runs: " I will " and " they shall." Jehovah swears it and the Son fulfils it. It is—it must be true. It must be sure, for "I AM" determines. "Hath he said, and shall he not do it? or hath he spoken, and shall he not make it good?" It is a sure covenant. I have sometimes said, if any man were about to build a bridge or a house, if he would leave me just one single stone or one timber to put where I liked, I would undertake that his house would fall down. Let me, if there is any one about to construct a bridge, have just simply the placing of one stone— I will select which stone it shall be—and I will defy him to build a bridge that shall stand. I should simply select the keystone, and then he might erect whatever he pleased and it should soon fall. Now, the Arminian's covenant is one that cannot stand, because there are one or two bricks in it (and that is putting it in the slightest form; I might have said, "because every stone in it," and that would be nearer the mark) that are dependent on the will of man. It is left to the will of the creature whether he will be saved or not. If he will not, there is no constraining influence that can master and overcome his will. There is no promise that any influence shall be strong enough to overcome him, according to the Arminian. So the question is left to man, and God the mighty Builder— though he put stone on stone, massive as the universe—yet may be defeated by his creature. Out upon such blasphemy! The whole structure, from beginning to end, is in the hand of God. The very terms and conditions of that covenant are become its seals and guarantees, seeing that Jesus has fulfilled them all. Its full accomplishment in every jot and tittle is sure, and must be fulfilled by Christ Jesus, whether man will or man will not. It is not the creature's covenant, it is the Creator's. It is not man's covenant, it is the Almighty's covenant, and he will carry it out and perform it, the will of man notwithstanding. For this is the very glory of grace—that man hates to be saved—that he is at enmity to God, yet God will have him redeemed—that God's covenant is, "you shall," and man's intention is, "I will not," and God's "shall" conquers man's "I will not." Almighty grace rides victoriously over the neck of freewill, and leads it captive, in glorious captivity to the all-conquering power of irresistible grace and love. It is a sure covenant, and therefore deserves the title of everlasting.

Furthermore, it is not only sure, but it is *immutable*. If it were not immutable, it could not be everlasting. That which changes passes away. We may be quite sure that anything that has the word "change" on it, will sooner or later die, and be put away as a thing of nought. But in the covenant everything is immutable. Whatever God has established must come to pass, and not word or line or letter can be altered. Whatever the Spirit voweth shall be done, and whatever God the Son promised hath been fulfilled and shall be consummated at the day of his appearing. Oh if we could believe that the sacred lines could be erased—that the covenant could be blotted and blurred, why then, my dear friends, we might lie down in despair. I have heard it said by some preachers, that when the Christian is holy, he is in the covenant; that when he sins, he is crossed out again; that when he repents, he is put in again, and then if he falls he is scratched out once more; and so he goes in and out of the door, as he would in and out of his own house. He goes in at one door and out of another. He is sometimes the child of God, and sometimes the child of the devil—sometimes an heir of heaven, and anon an heir of hell. And I know one man who went so far as to say that although a man might have persevered through grace for sixty years, yet should he fall away the last year of his life—if he should sin and die so, he would perish everlastingly, and all his faith, and all the love which God had manifested to him in the days gone by would go for nothing. I am very happy to say that such a notion of God is just the very notion I have of the devil. I could not believe in such a God, and could not bow down before him. A God that loves to-day and hates to-morrow; a God that gives a promise, and yet foreknows after all that man shall not see the promise fulfilled; a God that forgives and punishes—that justifies and afterwards executes—is a God that I cannot endure. He is not the God of the Scriptures, I am certain, for *he* is immutable, just, holy and true, and having loved his own, he will love them to the end, and if he hath given a promise to any man the promise shall be kept, and that man once in grace is in grace for ever, and shall without fail by-and-by enter into glory.

And then to finish up this point. The covenant is everlasting, because *it will never run itself out*. It will be fulfilled but it will stand firm. When Christ hath completed all, and brought every believer to heaven; when the Father hath seen all his people gathered in—the covenant, it is true, will come to a consummation, but not to a conclusion, for thus the covenant runs: The heirs of grace shall be blessed for ever, and as long as " for ever " lasts, this everlasting covenant will demand the happiness, the security, the glorification of every object of it.

III. Having thus noticed the everlasting character of the covenant, I conclude by the sweetest and most precious portion of the doctrine—the relation which the blood bears to it —THE BLOOD OF THE EVERLASTING COVENANT. The blood of Christ stands in a fourfold relationship to the covenant. *With regard to Christ*, his precious blood shed in Gethsemane, in Gabbatha and Golgotha, is *the fulfilment* of the covenant. By this blood sin is cancelled; by Jesus' agonies justice is satisfied, by his death the law is honoured; and by that precious blood in all its mediatorial efficacy, and in all its cleansing power, Christ fulfils all that he stipulated to do on the behalf of his people towards God. Oh, believer, look to the blood of Christ, and remember that there is Christ's part of the covenant carried out. And now, there remains nothing to be fulfilled but God's part, there is nothing for thee to do; Jesus has done it all; there is nothing for free will to supply; Christ has done everything that God can demand. The blood is the fulfilment of the debtor's side of the covenant, and now God becometh bound by his own solemn oath to show grace and mercy to all whom Christ has redeemed by his blood. With regard to the blood in another respect, it is *to God the Father the bond* of the covenant. When I see Christ dying on the cross, I see the everlasting God from that time, if I may use the term of him who ever must be free, bound by his own oath and covenant to carry out every stipulation. Does the covenant say: " A new heart will I give thee, and a right spirit will I put within thee?" It must be done, for Jesus died, and Jesus' death is the seal of the covenant. Does it say: " I will sprinkle pure water upon them and they shall be clean; from all their iniquities will I cleanse them?" Then it must be done, for Christ has fulfilled his part. And, therefore, now we can present the covenant no more as a thing of doubt, but as our claim on

God through Christ; and as we come humbly on our knees, pleading that covenant, our heavenly Father will not deny the promises contained therein, but will make every one of them yea and amen to us through the blood of Jesus Christ.

Then, again, the blood of the covenant has relation *to us as the objects* of the covenant, and that is its third light; it is not only a fulfilment as regards Christ, and a bond as regards his Father, but it is *an evidence* as regards ourselves. And here, dear brothers and sisters, let me speak affectionately to you. Are you relying wholly upon the blood? Has his blood—the precious blood of Christ—been laid to your conscience? Have you seen your sins pardoned, through his blood? Have you received forgiveness of sins through the blood of Jesus? Are you glorying in his sacrifice, and is his cross your only hope and refuge? Then you are in the covenant. Some men want to know whether they are elect. We cannot tell them unless they will tell us this. Dost thou believe? Is thy faith fixed on the precious blood? Then thou art in the covenant. And oh, poor sinner, if thou hast nothing to recommend thee; if thou art standing back and saying: "I dare not come! I am afraid! I am not in the covenant!" still Christ bids thee come. "Come unto *me*," saith he. "If thou canst not come to the covenant Father, come to the covenant Surety. Come unto *me* and I will give thee rest." And when thou hast come to him, and his blood has been applied to thee, doubt not but that in the red roll of election stands thy name. Canst thou read thy name in the bloody characters of a Saviour's atonement? Then shalt thou read it one day in the golden letters of the Father's election! He that believeth is elected. The blood is the symbol, the token, the earnest, the surety, the seal of the covenant of grace to thee. It must ever be the telescope through which thou canst look to see the things that are afar off. Thou canst not see thy election with the naked eye, but through the blood of Christ thou canst see it clear enough. Trust thou in the blood, poor sinner, and then the blood of the everlasting covenant is a proof that thou art an heir of heaven. Lastly, the blood stands in a relationship *to all three*, and here I may add that *the blood is the glory of all*. To the Son it is the fulfilment, to the Father the bond, to the sinner the evidence, and to all—to Father, Son and sinner—it is the common glory and the common boast. In this the Father is well pleased; in this the Son also, with joy, looks down and sees the purchase of his agonies; and in this must the sinner ever find his comfort and his everlasting song—" Jesus, thy blood and righteousness, are my glory, my song, for ever and ever!"

And now, my dear hearers, I have one question to ask, and I have done. Have you the hope that you are in the covenant? Have you put your trust in the blood? Though you imagine, perhaps, from what I have been saying, that the gospel is restricted, remember that the gospel is freely preached to all. The decree is limited, but the good news is as wide as the world. The good spell, the good news, is as wide as the universe. I tell it to every creature under heaven, because I am told to do so. The secret of God, which is to deal with the application, that is restricted to God's chosen ones, but not the message, for that is to be proclaimed to all nations. Now thou hast heard the gospel many and many a time in thy life. It runs thus: " This is a faithful saying, and worthy of all acceptation, that Christ Jesus came into the world to save sinners." Dost thou believe that? And is this thy hope—something like this: " I am a sinner. I trust Christ has died for me; I put my trust in the merit of his blood, and, sink or swim, I have no other hope but this.

> " Nothing in my hand I bring,
>   Simply to thy cross I cling."

Thou hast heard it; hast thou received it in thy heart, and laid hold on it; then thou art one of those in the covenant. And why should election frighten thee? If thou hast chosen Christ, depend upon it he has chosen thee. If thy tearful eye is looking to him, then his omniscient eye has long looked on thee; if thy heart loves him, his heart loves thee better than ever thou canst love, and if now thou art saying: " My father, thou shalt be the guide of my youth," I will tell thee a secret— he has been thy guide, and has brought thee to be what thou now art, a humble seeker, and he will be thy guide and bring thee safe at last. But art thou a proud, boastful, free-willer, saying: "I will repent and believe whenever I choose; I have as good a right to be saved as anybody, for I do my duty as well as others, and I shall doubtless get my reward "—if you are

4

claiming a universal atonement, which is to be received at the option of man's will, go and claim it, and you will be disappointed in your claim. You will find God will not deal with you on that ground at all, but will say: " Get thee hence, I never knew thee. He that cometh not to me through the Son cometh not at all." I believe the man who is not willing to submit to the electing love and sovereign grace of God, has great reason to question whether he is a Christian at all, for the spirit that kicks against that is the spirit of the devil, and the spirit of the unhumbled, unrenewed heart. May God take away out of your heart the enmity to his own precious truth, and reconcile you to it and then reconcile you to himself through THE BLOOD of his Son, which is the bond and seal of the everlasting covenant.

The Necessity of the Spirit's Work[1]

" And I will put my Spirit within you."—Ezekiel xxxvi. 27.

THE miracles of Christ are remarkable for one fact—namely, that they are none of them unnecessary. The pretended miracles of Mahomet, and of the church of Rome, even if they had been miracles, would have been pieces of folly. Suppose that Saint Denis had walked with his head in his hand after it had been cut off, what practical purpose would have been subserved thereby? He would certainly have been quite as well in his grave, for any practical good he would have conferred on men. The miracles of Christ were never unnecessary. They are not freaks of power; they are displays of power, it is true, but they all of them have a practical end. The same thing may be said of the promises of God. We have not one promise in the Scripture which may be regarded as a mere freak of grace. As every miracle was necessary, absolutely necessary, so is every promise that is given in the Word of God. And hence from the text that is before us, may I draw, and I think very conclusively, the argument, that if God in his covenant made with his people has promised to put his Spirit within them, it must be absolutely necessary that this promise should have been made, and it must be absolutely necessary also to our salvation that every one of us should receive the Spirit of God. This shall be the subject of this morning's discourse. I shall not hope to make it very interesting, except to those who are anxiously longing to know the way of salvation.

We start, then, by laying down this proposition—that the work of the Holy Spirit is absolutely necessary to us, if we would be saved.

1. In endeavouring to prove this, I would first of all make the remark that this is very manifest if we *remember what man is by nature.* Some say that man may of himself attain unto salvation—that if he hear the Word, it is in his power to

[1] Sunday morning, May 8th, 1859.

51

receive it, to believe it, and to have a saving change worked in him by it. To this we reply, you do not know what man is by nature, otherwise you would never have ventured upon such an assertion.   Holy Scripture tells us that man by nature is *dead* in trespasses and sins. It does not say that he is sick, that he is faint, that he has grown callous and hardened and seared, but it says he is absolutely dead. Whatever that term "death" means in connection with the body, that it means in connection with man's soul, viewing it in its relation to spiritual things. When the body is dead it is powerless; it is unable to do anything for itself; and when the soul of man is dead, in a spiritual sense, it must be, if there is any meaning in the figure, utterly and entirely powerless, and unable to do anything of itself or for itself. When ye shall see dead men raising themselves from their graves, when ye shall see them unwinding their own sheets, opening their own coffin lids, and walking down our streets alive and animate, as the result of their own power, then perhaps ye may believe that souls that are dead in sin may turn to God, may recreate their own natures, and may make themselves heirs of heaven, though before they were heirs of wrath. But mark, *not till then.* The drift of the gospel is, that man is dead in sin, and that divine life is God's gift; and you must go contrary to the whole of that drift, before you can suppose a man brought to know and love Christ, apart from the work of the Holy Spirit. The Spirit finds men as destitute of spiritual life as Ezekiel's dry bones; he brings bone to bone, and fits the skeleton together, and then he comes from the four winds and breathes into the slain, and they live, and stand upon their feet, an exceeding great army, and worship God. But apart from that, apart from the vivifying influence of the Spirit of God, men's souls must lie in the valley of dry bones, dead, and dead for ever.

But Scripture does not only tell us that man is dead in sin; it tells us something worse than this—namely, that he is utterly and entirely averse to everything that is good and right. "The carnal mind is enmity against God; for it is not subject to the law of God, neither indeed can be " (Romans viii. 7). Turn you all Scripture through, and you find continually the will of man described as being contrary to the things of God. What said Christ in that text so often quoted by the Arminian to disprove the very doctrine which it clearly states? What did Christ say to those who imagined that men would come without divine influence? He said, first: " No man can come unto me except the Father which hath sent me draw him "; but he said something more strong: " Ye *will not* come unto me that ye might have life." No man *will* come. Here lies the deadly mischief; not only that he is powerless to do good, but that he is powerful enough to do that which is wrong, and that his will is desperately set against everything that is right. Go, Arminian, and tell your hearers that they will come if they please, but know that your Redeemer looks you in the face, and tells you that you are uttering a lie. Men will *not* come. They never will come of themselves. You cannot induce them to come; you cannot force them to come by all your thunders, nor can you entice them to come by all your invitations. They *will not* come unto Christ that they may have life. Until the Spirit draw them, come they neither will, nor can.

Hence, then, from the fact that man's nature is hostile to the divine Spirit, that he hates grace, that he despises the way in which grace is brought to him, that it is contrary to his own proud nature to stoop to receive salvation by the deeds of another—hence it is necessary that the Spirit of God should operate to change the will, to correct the bias of the heart, to set man in a right track, and then give him strength to run in it. Oh! if ye read man and understand him, ye cannot help being sound on the point of the necessity of the Holy Spirit's work. It has been well remarked by a great writer, that he never knew a man who held any great theological error, who did not also hold a doctrine which diminished the depravity of man. The Arminian says man is fallen, it is true, but then he has power of will left, and that will is free; he can raise himself. He diminishes the desperate character of the fall of man. On the other hand, the Antinomian says, man cannot do anything, but that he is not at all responsible, and is not bound to do it, it is not his duty to believe, it is not his duty to repent. Thus, you see, he also diminishes the sinfulness of man; and has not right views of the fall. But once get the correct view, that man is utterly fallen, powerless, guilty, defiled, lost, condemned, and you *must* be sound on all points

of the great gospel of Jesus Christ.   Once believe man to be
what the Scripture says he is—once believe his heart to be depraved, his affections perverted, his understanding darkened,
his will perverse, and *you must* hold that if such a wretch as
that be saved, it must be the work of the Spirit of God, and of
the Spirit of God alone.

2. I have another proof ready to hand.   Salvation must be
the work of the Spirit in us, because *the means used in salvation are of themselves inadequate for the accomplishment of
the work*.   And what are the means of salvation?   Why, first
and foremost stands the preaching of the Word of God.   More
men are brought to Christ by preaching than by anything else;
for it is God's chief and first instrument.   This is the sword of
the Spirit, quick and powerful, to the dividing asunder of the
joints and marrow.   "It pleaseth God by the foolishness of
preaching to save them that believe."   But what is there in
preaching, by which souls are saved, that looks as if it would
be the means of saving souls?   I could point you to divers
churches and chapels into which you might step, and say:
"Here is a learned minister indeed, a man who would instruct
and enlighten the intellect"; you sit down, and you say:
"Well, if God means to work a great work he will use a
learned man like this."   But do you know any learned men
that are made the means of bringing souls to Christ, to any
great degree?   Go round your churches, if you please, and
look at them, and then answer the question.   Do you know
any great men—men great in learning and wisdom—who
have become spiritual fathers in our Israel?   Is it not a fact
that stares us in the face, that our fashionable preachers, our
eloquent preachers, our learned preachers, are just the most
useless men in creation for the winning of souls to Christ.
And where are souls born to God?   Why, in the house around
which the jeer and the scoff and the sneer of the world have
long gathered.   Sinners are converted under the man whose
eloquence is rough and homely, and who has nothing to commend him to his fellows, who has daily to fall on his knees and
confess his own folly, and when the world speaks worst of him,
feels that he deserves it all, since he is nothing but an earthen
vessel, in which God is pleased to put his heavenly treasure.
I will dare to say it, that in every age of the world the most

despised ministry has been the most useful; and I could find you at this day poor Primitive Methodist preachers who can scarce speak correct English, who have been the fathers of more souls, and have brought to Christ more than any one bishop on the bench. Why, the Lord hath been pleased always to make it so, that he will clothe with power the weak and the foolish, but he will not clothe with power those who, if good were done, might be led to ascribe the excellence of the power to their learning, their eloquence, or their position. Like the apostle Paul, it is every minister's business to glory in his infirmities. The world says: "Pshaw! upon your oratory; it is rough and rude and eccentric." Yes, 'tis even so, but we are content, for God blesses it. Then so much the better that it has infirmities in it; for now shall it be plainly seen that it is not of man or by man, but the work of God, and of God alone. It is said that once upon a time a man exceedingly curious desired to see the sword with which a mighty hero had fought some desperate battles; casting his eye along the blade, he said: "Well, I don't see much in this sword." "Nay," said the hero, " but you have not examined the arm that wields it." And so when men come to hear a successful minister, they are apt to say: "I do not see anything in him." No, but you have not examined the eternal arm that reaps its harvest with this sword of the Spirit. If ye had looked at the jaw-bone of the ass in Samson's hand, you would have said: "What! heaps on heaps with this?" No; bring out some polished blade; bring forth the Damascus steel! No; but God would have all the glory, and, therefore, not with the polished steel, but with the jaw-bone must Samson get the victory. So with ministers; God has usually blessed the weakest to do the most good. Well, now, does it not follow from this, that it must be the work of the Spirit? Because, if there be nothing in the instrument that can lead thereunto, is it not the work of the Spirit when the thing is accomplished? Let me just put it to you. Under the ministry dead souls are quickened, sinners are made to repent, the vilest of sinners are made holy, men who came determined not to believe are compelled to believe. Now, who does this? If you say the ministry does it, then I say farewell to your reason, because there is nothing in the successful ministry which would tend thereunto. It must be that the Spirit worketh in man through the ministry, or else such deeds would never be accomplished. You might as well expect to raise the dead by whispering in their ears, as hope to save souls by preaching to them, if it were not for the agency of the Spirit. Melancthon went out to preach, you know, without the Spirit of the Lord, and he thought he should convert all the people; but he found out at last that old Adam was too strong for young Melancthon, and he had to go back and ask for the help of the Holy Spirit or ever he saw a soul saved. I say, that the fact that the ministry is blessed, proves, since there is nothing in the ministry, that salvation must be the work of a higher power.

Other means, however, are made use of to bless men's souls. For instance, the two ordinances of Baptism and the Lord's Supper. They are both made a rich means of grace. But let me ask you, is there anything in baptism that can possibly bless anybody? Can immersion in water have the slightest tendency to be blessed to the soul? And then with regard to the eating of bread and the drinking of wine at the Lord's Supper, can it by any means be conceived by any rational man that there is anything in the mere piece of bread that we eat, or in the wine that we drink? And yet doubtless the grace of God does go with both ordinances for the confirming of the faith of those who receive them, and even for the conversion of those who look upon the ceremony. There must be something, then, beyond the outward ceremony; there must, in fact, be the Spirit of God, witnessing through the water, witnessing through the wine, witnessing through the bread, or otherwise none of these things could be means of grace to our souls. They could not edify, they could not help us to commune with Christ; they could not tend to the conviction of sinners, or to the establishment of saints. There must then, from these facts, be a higher, unseen, mysterious influence—the influence of the divine Spirit of God.

3. Let me again remind you, in the third place, that the absolute necessity of the work of the Holy Spirit in the heart may be clearly seen from this fact, that *all that has been done by God the Father, and all that has been done by God the Son must be ineffectual to us, unless the Spirit shall reveal these things to our souls.* We believe, in the first place, that God

the Father elects his people; from before all worlds he chooses them to himself; but let me ask you—what effect does the doctrine of election have upon any man, until the Spirit of God enters into him? How do I know whether God has chosen me from before the foundation of the world? How can I possibly know? Can I climb to heaven, and read the roll? Is it possible for me to force my way through the thick mists which hide eternity, and open the seven seals of the book, and read my name recorded there? Ah! no; election is a dead letter both in my consciousness and in any effect which it can produce upon me, until the Spirit of God calls me out of darkness into marvellous light. And then through my calling, I see my election, and knowing myself to be called of God, I know myself to have been chosen of God from before the foundation of the world. It is a precious thing—that doctrine of election —to a child of God. But what makes it precious? Nothing but the influence of the Spirit. Until the Spirit opens the eye to read, until the Spirit imparts the mystic secret, no heart can know its election. No angel ever revealed to any man that he was chosen of God; but the Spirit does it. He, by his divine workings, bears an infallible witness with our spirits that we are born of God; and then we are enabled to "read our title clear to mansions in the skies."

Look, again, at the covenant of grace. We know that there was a covenant made with the Lord Jesus Christ, by his Father, from before all worlds, and that in this covenant the persons of all his people were given to him, and were secured; but of what use, or of what avail is the covenant to us, until the Holy Spirit brings the blessings of the covenant to us? The covenant is, as it were, a lofty tree laden with fruit; if the Spirit doth not shake that tree and make the fruit fall therefrom until it comes to the level of our standing, how can we receive it? Bring hither any sinner and tell him there is a covenant of grace, what is he advantaged thereby? "Ah," says he, "I may not be included in it; my name may not be recorded there; I may not be chosen in Christ"; but let the Spirit of God dwell in his heart richly by faith and love which is in Christ Jesus, and that man sees the covenant, ordered in all things and sure, and he cries with David: "It is all my salvation and all my desire."

Take, again, the redemption of Christ. We know that Christ did stand in the room, place and stead of all his people, and that all those who shall appear in heaven, will appear there as an act of justice as well as of grace, seeing that Christ was punished in their room and stead, and that it would have been unjust if God punished them, seeing that he had punished Christ for them. We believe that, as Christ has paid all their debts, they have a right to their freedom in Christ—that as Christ has covered them with his righteousness, they are entitled to eternal life as much as if they had themselves been perfectly holy. But of what avail is this to me, until the Spirit takes of the things of Christ and shows them to me? What is Christ's blood to any of you, until you have received the Spirit of grace? You have heard the minister preach about the blood of Christ a thousand times, but you passed by; it was nothing to you that Jesus should die. You know that he did atone for sins that were not his own; but you only regarded it as a tale, perhaps, even an idle tale. But when the Spirit of God led you to the cross, and opened your eyes, and enabled you to see Christ crucified, ah, then there was something in the blood indeed. When his hand dipped the hyssop in the blood, and when it applied that blood to your spirit, then there was a joy and peace in believing, such as you had never known before. But ah, my hearer, Christ's dying is nothing to thee, unless thou hast a living Spirit within thee. Christ brings thee no advantage, saving, personal and lasting, unless the Spirit of God hath baptized thee in the fountain filled with his blood, and washed thee from head to foot therein.

I only mention these few out of the many blessings of the covenant, just to prove that they are none of them of any use to us, unless the Holy Spirit gives them to us. There hang the blessings on the nail—on the nail Christ Jesus; but we are short of stature; we cannot reach them; the Spirit of God takes them down and gives them to us, and there they are; they are ours. It is like the manna in the skies, far out of mortal reach; but the Spirit of God opens the windows of heaven, brings down the bread, and puts it to our lips, and enables us to eat. Christ's blood and righteousness are like wine stored in the wine-vat; but we cannot get thereat. The Holy Spirit

dips our vessel into this precious wine, and then we drink; but
without the Spirit we must die and perish just as much,
though the Father elect and the Son redeem, as though the
Father never had elected, and though the Son had never
bought us with his blood. The Spirit is absolutely necessary.
Without him neither the works of the Father, nor of the Son,
are of any avail to us.

4. This brings us to another point. *The experience of the
true Christian is a reality; but it never can be known and felt
without the Spirit of God.* For what is the experience of the
Christian? Let me just give a brief picture of some of its
scenes. There is a person come into this hall this morning—
one of the most reputable men in London. He has never com-
mitted himself in any outward vice; he has never been dishonest; but he is known as a staunch upright tradesman.
Now, to his astonishment, he is informed that he is a condemned, lost sinner, and just as surely lost as the thief who
died for his crimes upon the cross. Do you think that man
will believe it? Suppose, however, that he does believe it,
simply because he reads it in the Bible, do you think that man
will ever be made to feel it? I know you say: "Impossible!"
Some of you, even now, perhaps, are saying: "Well, I never
should!" Can you imagine that honourable, upright tradesman saying: "God be merciful to me, a sinner?" standing
side-by-side with the harlot and the swearer, and feeling in his
own heart as if he had been as guilty as they were, and using
just the same prayer, and saying: "Lord, save, or I perish."
You cannot conceive it, can you? It is contrary to nature that
a man who has been so good as he should put himself down
among the chief of sinners. Ah, but that will be done before
he will be saved; he must feel that before he can enter heaven.
Now, I ask, who can bring him to such a levelling experience
as that, but the Spirit of God? I know very well, proud
nature will not stoop to it. We are all aristocrats in our own
righteousness; we do not like to bend down and come among
common sinners. If we are brought there, it must be the
Spirit of God who casts us to the ground. Why, I know if any
one had told me that I should ever cry to God for mercy, and
confess that I had been the vilest of the vile, I should have
laughed in their face; I should have said: "Why, I have not

done anything particularly wrong; I have not hurt anybody."
And yet I know this very day I can take my place upon the
lowest form, and if I can get inside heaven I shall feel happy
to sit among the chief of sinners, and praise that Almighty love
which has saved even me from my sins. Now, what works this
humiliation of heart? Grace. It is contrary to nature for an
honest and an upright man in the eye of the world to feel
himself a lost sinner. It must be the Holy Spirit's work, or
else it never will be done. Well, after a man has been
brought here, can you conceive that man at last conscience-
stricken, and led to believe that his past life deserves the wrath
of God? His first thought would be: "Well, now, I will live
better than I ever have lived." He would say: "Now, I will
try and play the hermit, and pinch myself here and there, and
deny myself, and do penance; and in that way, by paying
attention to the outward ceremonies of religion, together with
a high moral character, I doubt not I shall blot out whatever
slurs and stains there have been." Can you suppose that man
brought at last to feel that, if ever he gets to heaven, he will
have to get there through the righteousness of another?
"Through the righteousness of another?" says he, "I don't
want to be rewarded for what another man does—not I. If I
go there, I will go there and take my chance; I will go there
through what I do myself. Tell me something to do, and I
will do it; I will be proud to do it, however humiliating it may
be, so that I may at last win the love and esteem of God!"
Now, can you conceive such a man as that brought to feel that
he can do nothing? That, good man as he thinks himself, he
cannot do anything whatever to merit God's love and favour;
and that if he goes to heaven he must go through what Christ
did? Just the same as the drunkard must go there through
the merits of Christ, so this moral man must enter into life,
having nothing about him but Christ's perfect righteousness,
and being washed in the blood of Jesus. We say that this is so
contrary to human nature, so diametrically opposed to all the
instincts of our poor fallen humanity, that nothing but the
Spirit of God can ever bring a man to strip himself of all self-
righteousness, and of all creature strength, and compel him
to rest and lean simply and wholly upon Jesus Christ the
Saviour.

These two experiences would be sufficient to prove the necessity of the Holy Spirit to make a man a Christian. But let me now describe a Christian as he is after his conversion. Trouble comes, storms of trouble, and he looks the tempest in the face, and says: " I know that all things work together for my good." His children die, the partner of his bosom is carried to the grave; he says: " The Lord gave and the Lord hath taken away, blessed be the name of the Lord." His farm fails, his crop is blighted; his business prospects are clouded, all seem to go, and he is left in poverty: he says: " Although the fig tree shall not blossom, neither shall fruit be in the vines; the labour of the olive shall fail, and the fields shall yield no meat; the flocks shall be cut off from the fold, and there shall be no herd in the stalls: yet I will rejoice in the Lord, I will joy in the God of my salvation." You see him next laid upon a sick bed himself, and when he is there, he says: " It is good for me that I have been afflicted, for before I was afflicted I went astray, but now have I kept thy Word." You see him approaching at last the dark valley of the shadow of death, and you hear him cry: " Yea, though I walk through the valley of the shadow of death, I will fear no evil; thy rod and thy staff comfort me, and thou thyself art with me." Now I ask you what makes this man calm in the midst of all these varied trials, and personal troubles, if it be not the Spirit of God? O, ye that doubt the influence of the Spirit, produce the like without him, go ye and die as Christians die, and live as they live, and if you can show the same calm resignation, the same quiet joy, and the same firm belief that adverse things shall nevertheless work together for good, then we may be perhaps at liberty to resign the point, and not till then. The high and noble experience of a Christian in times of trial and suffering, proves that there must be the operation of the Spirit of God.

But look at the Christian, too, in his joyous moments. He is rich. God has given him all his heart's desire on earth. Look at him; he says: " I do not value these things at all, except as they are the gift of God; I sit loose by them all, and notwithstanding this house and home, and all these comforts, ' I am willing to depart and be with Christ, which is far better.' It is true, I want nothing here on earth; but still I feel that to die would be gain to me, even though I left all these." He holds earth loosely; he does not grasp it with a tight hand, but looks upon it all as dust—a thing which is to pass away. He takes but little pleasure therein, saying:

> " I've no abiding city here,
> I seek a city out of sight."

Mark that man; he has plenty of room for pleasures in this world, but he drinks out of a higher cistern. His pleasure springs from things unseen; his happiest moments are when he can shut all these good things out, and when he can come to God as a poor guilty sinner, and through Christ can enter into fellowship with him, and rise into nearness of access and confidence, and make a bold approach to the throne of the heavenly grace. Now, what is it that keeps a man who has all these mercies from setting his heart upon the earth? This is a wonder indeed, that a man who has gold and silver, and flocks and herds, should not make these his god, but that he should still say:

> " There's nothing round this spacious earth
>   That suits my large desire;
> To boundless joy and solid mirth
>   My nobler thoughts aspire."

These are not my treasure; my treasure is in heaven, and in heaven only. What can do this? No mere moral virtue. No doctrine of the Stoic ever brought a man to such a pass as that. No, it must be the work of the Spirit, and the work of the Spirit alone, that can lead a man to live in heaven, while there is a temptation to him to live on earth. I do not wonder that a poor man looks forward to heaven; he has nothing to look upon on earth. When there is a thorn in the nest, I do not wonder that the lark flies up, for there is no rest for him below. When you are beaten and chafed by trouble, no wonder you say:

> " Jerusalem ! my happy home !
>   Name ever dear to me;
> When shall my labours have an end,
>   In joy, and peace, and thee?"

But the greatest wonder is, if you line the Christian's nest never so softly, if you give him all the mercies of this life, you still cannot keep him from saying:

> " To Jesus, the crown of my hope,
> My soul is in haste to be gone;
> Oh bear me, ye cherubim, up,
> And waft me away to his throne."

5. And now, last of all, the acts, *the acceptable acts of the Christian's life, cannot be performed without the Spirit*; and hence, again, the necessity for the Spirit of God. The first act of the Christian's life is repentance. Have you ever tried to repent? If so, if you tried without the Spirit of God, you know that to urge a man to repent without the promise of the Spirit to help him, is to urge him to do an impossibility. A rock might as soon weep, and a desert might as soon blossom, as a sinner repent of his own accord. If God should offer heaven to man, simply upon the terms of repentance of sin, heaven would be as impossible as it is by good works; for a man can no more repent of himself, than he can perfectly keep God's law; for repentance involves the very principle of perfect obedience to the law of God. It seems to me that in repentance there is the whole law solidified and condensed; and if a man can repent of himself then there is no need of a Saviour, he may as well go to heaven up the steep sides of Sinai at once.

Faith is the next act in the divine life. Perhaps you think faith very easy; but if you are ever brought to feel the burden of sin you would not find it quite so light a labour. If you are ever brought into deep mire, where there is no standing, it is not so easy to put your feet on a rock, when the rock does not seem to be there. I find faith just the easiest thing in the world when there is nothing to believe; but when I have room and exercise for my faith, then I do not find I have so much strength to accomplish it. As I talked one day with a countryman, he used this figure: " In the middle of winter I sometimes think how well I could mow; and in early spring I think, oh! how I would like to reap; I feel just ready for it; but when mowing time comes, and when reaping time comes, I find I have not strength to spare." So when you have no troubles, couldn't you mow them down at once? When you have no work to do, couldn't you do it? But when work and trouble come, you find how difficult it is. Many Christians are like the stag, who talked to itself, and said: "Why should I run away from the dogs? Look what a fine pair of horns I've got and look what heels I've got too; I might do these hounds some mischief. Why not let me stand and show them what I can do with my antlers? I can keep off any quantity of dogs." No sooner did the dogs bark, than off the stag went. So with us. "Let sin arise," we say, "we will soon rip it up, and destroy it; let trouble come, we will soon get over it"; but when sin and trouble come, we then find what our weakness is. Then we have to cry for the help of the Spirit; and through him we can do all things, though without him we can do nothing at all.

In all the acts of the Christian's life, whether it be the act of consecrating one's self to Christ, or the act of daily prayer, or the act of constant submission, or preaching the gospel, or ministering to the necessities of the poor, or comforting the desponding, in all these the Christian finds his weakness and his powerlessness, unless he is clothed about with the Spirit of God. Why, I have been to see the sick at times, and I have thought how I would like to comfort them; and I could not get a word out that was worth their hearing, or worth my saying; and my soul has been in agony to be the means of comforting the poor sick desponding brother, but I could do nothing, and I came out of the chamber, and half wished I had never been to see a sick person in my life: I had so learned my own folly. So has it been full often in preaching. You get a sermon up, study it, and come and make the greatest mess of it that can possibly be. Then you say: "I wish I had never preached at all." But all this is to show us, that neither in comforting nor in preaching can one do anything right, unless the Spirit work in us to will and to do of his own good pleasure. Everything, moreover, that we do without the Spirit is unacceptable to God; and whatever we do under his influence, however we may despise it, is not despised of God, for he never despises his own work, and the Spirit never can look upon what he works in us with any other view than that of complacency and delight. If the Spirit helps me to groan, then God must accept the groaner. If thou couldst pray the best prayer in the world, without the Spirit, God would have nothing to do with it; but if thy prayer be broken and lame and limping, if the Spirit made it, God will look upon it, and say, as he did upon the works of creation: " It is very good"; and he will accept it.

And now let me conclude by asking this question. My hearer, then have you the Spirit of God in you? You have some religion, most of you, I dare say. Well, of what kind is it? Is it a home-made article? Did you make yourself what you are? Then, if so, you are a lost man up to this moment. If, my hearer, you have gone no further than you have walked yourself, you are not on the road to heaven yet, you have got your face turned the wrong way; but if you have received something which neither flesh nor blood could reveal to you, if you have been led to do the very thing which you once hated, and to love that thing which you once despised, and to despise that on which your heart and your pride were once set, then, soul, if this be the Spirit's work, rejoice; for where he hath begun the good work, he will carry it on. And you may know whether it is the Spirit's work by this. Have you been led to Christ, and away from self? Have you been led away from all feelings, from all doings, from all willings, from all prayings, as the ground of your trust and your hope, and have you been brought nakedly to rely upon the finished work of Christ? If so, this is more than human nature ever taught any man; this is a height to which human nature never climbed. The Spirit of God has done that, and he will never leave what he has once begun, but thou shalt go from strength to strength, and thou shalt stand among the blood-washed throng, at last complete in Christ, and accepted in the beloved. But if you have not the Spirit of Christ, you are none of his. May the Spirit lead you to your chamber now to weep, now to repent, and now to look to Christ, and may you now have a divine life implanted, which neither time nor eternity shall be able to destroy. God hear this prayer, and send us away with a blessing, for Jesus' sake. Amen.

Predestination and Calling[1]

"Moreover whom he did predestinate, them he also called."
—Romans viii. 30.

THE great book of God's decrees is fast closed against the curiosity of man. Vain man would be wise; he would break the seven seals thereof, and read the mysteries of eternity. But this cannot be; the time has not yet come when the book shall be opened, and even then the seals shall not be broken by mortal hand, but it shall be said: "The lion of the tribe of Judah hath prevailed to open the book and break the seven seals thereof."

> "Eternal Father, who shall look
> Into thy secret will?
> *None but the Lamb shall take the book,*
> *And open every seal.*"

None but he shall ever unroll that sacred record and read it to the assembled world. How then am I to know whether I am predestinated by God unto eternal life or no? It is a question in which my eternal interests are involved; am I among that unhappy number who shall be left to live in sin and reap the due reward of their iniquity; or do I belong to that goodly company, who albeit that they have sinned shall nevertheless be washed in the blood of Christ, and shall in white robes walk the golden streets of paradise? Until this question be answered my heart cannot rest, for I am intensely anxious about it. My eternal destiny infinitely more concerns me than all the affairs of time. Tell me, oh, tell me, if ye know, seers and prophets, is my name recorded in that book of life? Am I one of those who are ordained unto eternal life, or am I to be left to follow my own lusts and passions, and to destroy my own soul? Oh! man, there is an answer to thy enquiry; the book cannot be opened, but God himself hath published many a page thereof. He hath not published the page whereon the actual *names* of the redeemed are written; but that page

[1] Sunday morning, March 6th, 1859.

66

of the sacred decree whereon their *character* is recorded is published in his Word, and shall be proclaimed to thee this day. The sacred record of God's hand is this day published everywhere under heaven, and he that hath an ear let him hear what the Spirit saith unto him. O my hearer, by thy name I know thee not, and by thy name God's Word doth not declare thee, but by thy character thou mayest read thy name; and if thou hast been a partaker of the calling which is mentioned in the text, then mayest thou conclude beyond a doubt that thou art among the predestinated: "For whom he did predestinate, them he also called." And if thou be called, it follows as a natural inference thou art predestinated.

Now, in considering this solemn subject, let me remark that there are two kinds of callings mentioned in the Word of God. The first is the *general call*, which is in the gospel sincerely given to everyone that heareth the word. The duty of the minister is to call souls to Christ, he is to make no distinction whatever: "Go ye into all the world, and preach the gospel *to every creature*." The trumpet of the gospel sounds aloud to every man in our congregations: "Ho, everyone that thirsteth, come ye to the waters, and he that hath no money; come ye, buy and eat; yea, come, buy wine and milk without money and without price." "Unto you, O men, I call; and my voice is to the sons of man" (Prov. viii. 4). This call is sincere on God's part; but man by nature is so opposed to God, that this call is never effectual, for man disregards it, turns his back upon it, and goes his way, caring for none of these things. But mark, although this call be rejected, man is without excuse in the rejection; the universal call has in it such authority, that the man who will not obey it shall be without excuse in the day of judgment. When thou art commanded to believe and repent, when thou art exhorted to flee from the wrath to come, the sin lies on thy own head if thou dost despise the exhortation, and reject the commandment. And this solemn text drops an awful warning: "How shall ye escape if ye neglect so great salvation" But I repeat it, this universal call is rejected by man; it is a call, but it is not attended with the divine force and energy of the Holy Spirit in such a degree as to make it an unconquerable call; consequently men perish, even though they have the universal call of the gospel ringing in their ears.

The bell of God's house rings every day, sinners hear it, but they put their fingers in their ears, and go their way, one to his farm, and another to his merchandise, and though they are bidden and are called to the wedding (Luke xiv. 16, 17, 18), yet they will not come, and by not coming they incur God's wrath, and he declareth of such: " None of those men which were bidden shall taste of my supper " (Luke xiv. 24). The call of our text is of a different kind; it is not a universal call, it is a special, particular, personal, discriminating, efficacious, unconquerable call. This call is sent to the predestinated, and to them only; they by grace hear the call, obey it and receive it. These are they who can now say: " Draw us, and we will run after thee."

In preaching of this call this morning, I shall divide my sermon into three brief parts: first, I shall give *illustrations of the call*; secondly, we shall come to *examine whether we have been called*; and then thirdly, *what delightful consequences flow therefrom*. Illustration, examination, consolation.

I. First, then, for ILLUSTRATION. In illustrating the effectual call of grace, which is given to the predestined ones, I must first use the picture of Lazarus. See you that stone rolled at the mouth of the sepulchre? Much need is there for the stone that it should be well secured, for within the sepulchre there is a putrid corpse. The sister of that corrupt body stands at the side of the tomb, and she says: " Lord, by this time he stinketh, for he hath been dead four days." This is the voice of reason and of nature. Martha is correct; but by Martha's side there stands a man who, despite all his lowliness, is very God of very God. " Roll ye away the stone," saith he, and it is done; and now, listen to him; he cries: " Lazarus, come forth! " That cry is directed to a mass of putridity, to a body that has been dead four days, and in which the worms have already held carnival; but, strange to say, from that tomb there comes a living man; that mass of corruption has been quickened into life, and out he comes, wrapped about with grave clothes, and having a napkin about his head. " Loose him and let him go," saith the Redeemer; and then he walks in all the liberty of life. The effectual call of grace is precisely similar; the sinner is dead in sin; he is not only in sin but *dead* in sin, without any power whatever to give to himself the life of grace. Nay, he is not only dead, but he is corrupt; his lusts, like the worms, have crept into him, a foul stench riseth up into the nostrils of justice, God abhorreth him, and justice crieth: " Bury the dead out of my sight, cast it into the fire, let it be consumed." Sovereign Mercy comes, and there lies this unconscious, lifeless mass of sin; Sovereign Grace cries, either by the minister, or else directly without any agency, by the Spirit of God: " Come forth! " and that man lives. Does he contribute anything to his new life? Not he; his life is given solely by God. He was dead, absolutely dead, rotten in his sin; the life is given when the call comes, and, in obedience to the call, the sinner comes forth from the grave of his lust, begins to live a new life, even the life eternal, which Christ gives to his sheep.

"Well," cries one, " but what are the words which Christ uses when he calls a sinner from death?" Why, the Lord may use any words. It was not long ago there came into this hall a man who was without God and without Christ, and the simple reading of the hymn—

" Jesus, lover of my soul,"

was the means of his quickening. He said within himself: "Does Jesus love me? then I must love him," and he was quickened in that self-same hour. The words which Jesus uses are various in different cases. I trust that even while I am speaking this morning, Christ may speak through me, and some word that may fall from my lips, unpremeditated and almost without design, shall be sent of God as a message of life unto some dead and corrupt heart here, and some man who has lived in sin hitherto, shall now live to righteousness, and live to Christ. That is the first illustration I will give you of what is meant by effectual calling. It finds the sinner dead, it gives him life, and he obeys the call of life and lives.

But let us consider a second phase of it. You will remember while the sinner is dead in sin, he is alive enough so far as any opposition to God may be concerned. He is powerless to obey, but he is mighty enough to resist the call of divine grace. I may illustrate it in the case of Saul of Tarsus: this proud Pharisee abhors the Lord Jesus Christ; he has seized upon every follower of Jesus who comes within his grasp; he has haled men and women to prison; with the avidity of a miser who hunts after gold, he has hunted after the precious life of Christ's disciple, and having exhausted his prey in Jerusalem, he seeks letters and goes off to Damascus upon the same bloody errand. Speak to him on the road, send out the apostle Peter to him, let Peter say: "Saul, why dost thou oppose Christ? The time shall come when thou shalt yet be his disciple." Paul would turn round and laugh him to scorn: "Get thee gone, thou fisherman, get thee gone—*I* a disciple of that impostor Jesus of Nazareth! Look here, this is my confession of faith; here will I hale thy brothers and thy sisters to prison, and beat them in the synagogue and compel them to blaspheme, and even hunt them to death, for my breath is threatening, and my heart is as fire against Christ." Such a scene did not occur, but had there been any remonstrance given by men you may easily conceive that such would have been Saul's answer. But Christ determined that he would call the man. Oh, what an enterprise! Stop HIM? Why he is going fast onward in his mad career. But lo, a light shines round about him and he falls to the ground, and he hears a voice crying: "Saul, Saul, why persecutest thou me; it is hard for thee to kick against the pricks." Saul's eyes are filled with tears, and then again with scales of darkness, and he cries: "Who art thou?" And a voice calls: "I am Jesus, whom thou persecutest." It is not many minutes before he begins to feel his sin in having persecuted Jesus, nor many hours ere he receives the assurance of his pardon, and not many days ere he who persecuted Christ, stands up to preach, with vehemence and eloquence unparalleled, the very cause which he once trod beneath his feet. See what effectual calling can do. If God should choose this morning to call the hardest-hearted wretch within hearing of the gospel, he must obey. Let God call—a man may resist, but he cannot resist effectually. Down thou shalt come, sinner, if God cries *down*; there is no standing when he would have thee fall. And mark, every man that is saved, is always saved by an overcoming call which he cannot withstand; he may resist it for a time, but he cannot resist so as to overcome it, he *must* give way, he *must* yield when God speaks. If God says: "Let there be light," the impenetrable darkness gives way to light; if he says: "Let there be grace," unutterable sin

gives way, and the hardest-hearted sinner melts before the fire
of effectual calling.

I have thus illustrated the call in two ways, by the state of
the sinner in his sin, and by the omnipotence which over-
whelms the resistance which he offers. And now another case.
The effectual call may be illustrated *in its sovereignty* by the
case of Zacchaeus. Christ is entering into Jericho to preach.
There is a publican living in it, who is a hard, griping, grasp-
ing, miserly extortioner. Jesus Christ is coming in to call
some one, for it is written he must abide in some man's house.
Would you believe it, that the man whom Christ intends to
call is the worst man in Jericho—the extortioner? He is a
little short fellow, and he cannot see Christ, though he has a
great curiosity to look at him; so he runs before the crowd and
climbs up a sycamore tree, and thinking himself quite safe
amid the thick foliage, he waits with eager expectation to see
this wonderful man who had turned the world upside down.
Little did he think that he was to turn him also. The Saviour
walks along preaching and talking with the people until he
comes under the sycamore tree, then lifting up his eyes, he
cries: "Zacchaeus, make haste and come down, for to-day I
must abide in thy house." The shot took effect, the bird fell,
down came Zacchaeus, invited the Saviour to his house, and
proved that he was really called not by the voice merely but
by grace itself, for he said: "Behold, Lord, the half of my
goods I give unto the poor, and if I have taken anything from
any man by false accusation, I restore unto him fourfold";
and Jesus said: "This day is salvation come to this house."
Now why call *Zacchaeus*? There were many better men in
the city than he. Why call him? Simply because the call of
God comes to unworthy sinners. There is nothing in man
that can deserve this call; nothing in the best of men that can
invite it; but God quickeneth whom he will, and when he
sends that call, though it come to the vilest of the vile, down
they come speedily and swiftly; they come down from the tree
of their sin, and fall prostrate in penitence at the feet of Jesus
Christ.

But now to illustrate this call in its effects, we remind you
that Abraham is another remarkable instance of effectual calling. "Now the Lord had said unto Abraham, get thee out of

thy country, and from thy kindred, and from thy father's house, unto a land that I will show thee," and " by faith, Abraham, when he was called to go out into a place which he should after receive for an inheritance, obeyed, and he went out, not knowing whither he went." Ah! poor Abraham, as the world would have had it, what a trial his call cost him! He was happy enough in the bosom of his father's household, but idolatry crept into it, and when God called Abraham, he called him alone and blessed him out of Ur of the Chaldees, and said to him: " Go forth, Abraham! " and he went forth, not knowing whither he went. Now, when effectual calling comes into a house and singles out a man, that man will be compelled to go forth without the camp, bearing Christ's reproach. He must come out from his very dearest friends, from all his old acquaintances, from those friends with whom he used to drink and swear and take pleasure; he must go straight away from them all, to follow the Lamb whithersoever he goeth. What a trial to Abraham's faith, when he had to leave all that was so dear to him, and go he knew not whither! And yet God had a goodly land for him, and intended greatly to bless him. Man! if thou art called, if thou art called truly, there will be a going out, and a going out alone. Perhaps some of God's professed people will leave you; you will have to go without a solitary friend—maybe you will even be deserted by Sarah herself, and you may be a stranger in a strange land, a solitary wanderer, as all your fathers were. Ah! but if it be an effectual call, and if salvation shall be the result thereof, what matters it though thou dost go to heaven alone? Better to be a solitary pilgrim to bliss, than one of the thousands who throng the road to hell.

I will have one more illustration. When effectual calling comes to a man, at first he may not know that it is effectual calling. You remember the case of Samuel: the Lord called Samuel, and he arose and went to Eli, and he said: " Here am I, for thou calledst me." Eli said: " I called not, lie down again. And he went and lay down." The second time the Lord called him, and said: " Samuel, Samuel," and he arose again, and went to Eli, and said: " Here am I, for thou didst call me," and then it was that Eli, not Samuel, first of all perceived that the Lord had called the child. And when Samuel knew it was the Lord, he said: "Speak; for thy servant heareth." When the work of grace begins in the heart, the man is not always clear that it is God's work: he is impressed under the minister, and perhaps he is rather more occupied with the impression than with the agent of the impression; he says: "I know not how it is, but I have been called: Eli, the minister, has called me." And perhaps he goes to Eli to ask what he wants with him. "Surely," said he, "the minister knew me, and spoke something personally to me, because he knew my case." And he goes to Eli, and it is not till afterwards, perhaps, that he finds that Eli had nothing to do with the impression, but that the Lord had called him. I know this—I believe God was at work with my heart for years before I knew anything about him. I knew there was a work; I knew I prayed and cried and groaned for mercy, but I did not know that was the Lord's work; I half thought it was my own. I did not know till afterwards, when I was led to know Christ as all my salvation, and all my desire, that *the Lord* had called the child, for this could not have been the result of nature, it must have been the effect of grace. I think I may say to those who are the beginners in the divine life, so long as your call is real, rest assured it is divine. If it is a call that will suit the remarks which I am about to give you in the second part of the discourse, even though you may have thought that God's hand is not in it, rest assured that it is, for nature could never produce effectual calling. If the call be effectual, and you are brought out and brought in—brought out of sin and brought to Christ, brought out of death into life, and out of slavery into liberty, then, though thou canst not see God's hand in it, yet it is there.

II. I have thus illustrated effectual calling. And now as a matter of EXAMINATION let each man judge himself by certain characteristics of heavenly calling which I am about to mention. If in your Bible you turn to 2 Timothy i. 9, you will read these words: "Who hath saved us, and called us with an holy calling." Now here is the first touchstone by which we may try our calling—many are called but few are chosen, because there are many kinds of call, but the true call, and that only, answers to the description of the text. It is "an holy calling, not according to our works, but according to his own purpose and grace, which was given us in Christ Jesus before the world began." This calling forbids all trust in our own doings and conducts us to Christ alone for salvation, but it afterwards purges us from dead works to serve the living and true God. If you are living in sin, you are not called; if you can still continue as you were before your pretended conversion, then it is no conversion at all; that man who is called in his drunkenness, will forsake his drunkenness; men may be called in the midst of sin, but they will not continue in it any longer. Saul was anointed to be king when he was seeking his father's asses; and many a man has been called when he has been seeking his own lust, but he will leave the asses, and leave the lust, when once he is called. Now, by this shall ye know whether ye be called of God or no. If ye continue in sin, if ye walk according to the course of this world, according to the spirit that worketh in the children of disobedience, then are ye still dead in your trespasses and your sins; but as he that hath called you is holy, so must ye be holy. Can ye say: "Lord, thou knowest all things, thou knowest that I desire to keep all thy commandments, and to walk blamelessly in thy sight. I know that my obedience cannot save me, but I long to obey. There is nothing that pains me so much as sin; I desire to be quit and rid of it: Lord help me to be holy?" Is that the panting of thy heart? Is that the tenor of thy life towards God, and towards his law? Then, beloved, I have reason to hope that thou hast been called of God, for it is a holy calling wherewith God doth call his people.

Another text. In Philippians iii. 13, 14, you find these words: "Forgetting those things which are behind, and reaching forth unto those which are before, I press towards the mark for the prize of the *high* calling of God in Christ Jesus." Is then your calling a high calling, has it lifted up your heart, and set it upon heavenly things? Has it lifted up your hopes, to hope no longer for things that are on earth, but for things that are above? Has it lifted up your tastes, so that they are no longer grovelling, but you choose the things that are of God? Has it lifted up your desires, so that you are panting not for earthly things, but for the things that are not seen and are eternal? Has it lifted up the constant tenor of your life, so that you spend your life with God in prayer, in praise and in thanksgiving, and can no longer be satisfied with the low and mean pursuits which you followed in the days of your ignorance? Recollect, if you are truly called, it is a high calling, a calling from on high, and a calling that lifts up your heart, and raises it to the high things of God, eternity, heaven and holiness.

In Hebrews iii. 1, you find this sentence: " Holy brethren partakers of the *heavenly* calling." Here is another test. Heavenly calling means a call *from* heaven. Have you been called, not of man but of God? Can you now detect in your calling, the hand of God, and the voice of God? If man alone call thee, thou art uncalled. Is thy calling of God? And is it a call *to* heaven as well as from heaven? Can you heartily say that you can never rest satisfied till you—

> ". . . behold his face
> And never, never sin,
> But from the rivers of his grace,
> Drink endless pleasures in."

Man, unless thou art a stranger here, and heaven is thy home, thou hast not been called with a heavenly calling, for those who have been so called, declare that they look for a city which hath foundations, whose builder and maker is God, and they themselves are strangers and pilgrims upon the earth.

There is another test. Let me remind you, that there is a passage in Scripture which may tend very much to your edification, and help you in your examination. Those who are called, are men who, before the calling, groaned in sin. What says Christ?: " I came not to call the righteous, but sinners to repentance." Now, if I cannot say the first things because of diffidence, though they be true, yet can I say this, that I feel myself to be a sinner, that I loathe my sinnership, that I detest my iniquity, that I feel I deserve the wrath of God on account of my transgressions? If so, then I have a hope that I may be among the called host whom God has predestinated. He has called not the righteous but sinners to repentance. Self-righteous man, I can tell thee in the tick of a clock, whether thou hast any evidence of election. I tell thee—No; Christ never called the righteous; and if he has not called thee, and if he never does call thee, thou art not elect, and thou and thy self-righteousness must be subject to the wrath of God, and cast away eternally. Only the sinner, the awakened sinner,

can be at all assured that he has been called, and even he, as
he gets older in grace, must look for those higher marks of the
high, heavenly and holy calling in Christ Jesus.

As a further test—keeping close to Scripture this morning,
for when we are dealing with our own state before God there is
nothing like giving the very words of Scripture—we are told
in the first epistle of Peter, the second chapter, and the ninth
verse, that God hath called us out of darkness into marvellous
light. Is that your call? Were you once darkness in regard
to Christ; and has marvellous light manifested to you a marvellous Redeemer, marvellously strong to save? Say soul,
canst thou honestly declare that thy past life was darkness and
that thy present state is light in the Lord? "For ye were
sometime darkness, but now are ye light in the Lord: walk as
children of the light." That man is not called who cannot
look back upon darkness, ignorance and sin, and who cannot
now say that he knows more than he did know, and enjoys at
times the light of knowledge, and the comfortable light of
God's countenance.

Yet again. Another test of calling is to be found in Galatians, the fifth chapter, and the thirteenth verse: "Brethren,
ye have been called into liberty." Let me ask myself again
this question, Have the fetters of my sin been broken off, and
am I God's free man? Have the manacles of justice been
snapped, and am I delivered—set free by him who is the great
ransomer of spirits? The slave is not called. It is the free
man that has been brought out of Egypt, who proves that he
has been called of God and is precious to the heart of the Most
High.

And yet once more, another precious means of test in the
first of Corinthians, the first chapter, and the ninth verse.
"God is faithful by whom ye were called into the fellowship
of his Son, Jesus Christ our Lord." Do I have fellowship with
Christ? Do I converse with him, commune with him? Do I
suffer *with* him, suffer *for* him? Do I sympathise with him in
his objects and aims? Do I love what he loves; do I hate what
he hates? Can I bear his reproach; can I carry his cross; do I
tread in his steps; do I serve his cause, and is it my grandest
hope that I shall see his kingdom come, that I shall sit upon
his throne, and reign with him? If so, then am I called with

the effectual calling, which is the work of God's grace, and is the sure sign of my predestination.

Let me say now, before I turn from this point, that it is possible for a man to know whether God has called him or not, and he may know it too beyond a doubt. He may know it as surely as if he read it with his own eyes; nay, he may know it more surely than that, for if I read a thing with my eyes, even my eyes may deceive me, the testimony of sense may be false, but *the testimony of the Spirit must be true.* We have the witness of the Spirit within, bearing witness with our spirits that we are born of God. There is such a thing on earth as an infallible assurance of our election. Let a man once get that, and it will anoint his head with fresh oil, it will clothe him with the white garment of praise, and put the song of the angel into his mouth. Happy, happy man! who is fully assured of his interest in the covenant of grace, in the blood of atonement, and in the glories of heaven! Such men there are here this very day. Let them " rejoice in the Lord alway, and again, I say rejoice."

What would some of you give if you could arrive at this assurance? Mark, if you anxiously desire to know, you may know. If your heart pants to read its title clear it shall do so ere long. No man ever desired Christ in his heart with a living and longing desire, who did not find him sooner or later. If thou hast a desire, God has given it thee. If thou pantest, and criest, and groanest after Christ, even this is his gift; bless him for it. Thank him for little grace, and ask him for great grace. He has given thee hope, ask for faith; and when he gives thee faith, ask for assurance; and when thou gettest assurance, ask for full assurance; and when thou hast obtained full assurance, ask for enjoyment; and when thou hast enjoyment, ask for glory itself; and he shall surely give it thee in his own appointed season.

III. I now come to finish up with CONSOLATION. Is there anything here that can console me? Oh, yes, rivers of consolation flow from my calling. For, first, if I am called then I am predestinated, there is no doubt about it. The great scheme of salvation is like those chains which we sometimes see at horse-ferries. There is a chain on this side of the river fixed into a staple, and the same chain is fixed into a staple at the other side, but the greater part of the chain is for the most part under water, and you cannot see it: you only see it as the boat moves on, and as the chain is drawn out of the water by the force that propels the boat. If to-day I am enabled to say I am called, then my boat is like the ferry-boat in the middle of the stream. I can see that part of the chain, which is named "calling," but blessed be God, that is joined to the side that is called "election," and I may be also quite clear that it is joined on to the other side, the glorious end of "glorification." If I be called I must have been elected, and I need not doubt that. God never tantalized a man by calling him by grace effectually, unless he had written that man's name in the Lamb's book of life. Oh, what a glorious doctrine is that of election, when a man can see himself to be elect. One of the reasons why many men kick against it is this, they are afraid it hurts them. I never knew a man yet who had a reason to believe that he himself was chosen of God, who hated the doctrine of election. Men hate election just as thieves hate Chubb's patent locks; because they cannot get at the treasure themselves, they therefore hate the guard which protects it. Now election shuts up the precious treasury of God's covenant blessings for his children—for penitents, for seeking sinners. These men will not repent, will not believe; they will not go God's way, and then they grumble and growl and fret and fume because God has locked the treasure up against them. Let a man once believe that all the treasure within is his, and then the stouter the bolt and the surer the lock the better for him. Oh, how sweet it is to believe our names were on Jehovah's heart, and graven on Jesus' hands before the universe had a being! May not this electrify a man with joy, and make him dance for very mirth?

"Chosen of God ere time began."

Come on, slanderers! Rail on as pleases you. Come on, thou world in arms! Cataracts of trouble, descend if you will, and you, ye floods of affliction, roll if so it be ordained, for God has written my name in the book of life. Firm as this rock I stand, though nature reels and all things pass away. What consolation then to be called: for if I am called, then I am predestinated. Come let us wonder at the sovereignty which has called us, and let us remember the words of the apostle: " For ye see your calling, brethren, how that not many wise men after the flesh, not many mighty, not many noble, are called: but God hath chosen the foolish things of the world to confound the wise; and God hath chosen the weak things of the world, to confound the things which are mighty; and base things of the world, and things which are despised, hath God chosen, yea, and things which are not, to bring to nought things that are: that no flesh should glory in his presence. But of him are ye in Christ Jesus, who of God is made unto us wisdom and righteousness and sanctification and redemption: that, according as it is written, he that glorieth, let him glory in the Lord."

A second consolation is drawn from the grand truth, that if a man be called he will certainly be saved at last. To prove that, however, I will refer you to the express words of Scripture (Romans xi. 29): " The gifts and calling of God are without repentance." He never repents of what he gives, nor of what he calls. And indeed this is proved by the very chapter out of which we have taken our text. " Whom he did predestinate, them he also called; and whom he called, them he also justified; and whom he justified, them he also glorified," everyone of them. Now, believer, thou mayest be very poor and very sick and very much unknown and despised, but sit thee down and review thy calling this morning, and the consequences that flow from it. As sure as thou art God's called child to-day, thy poverty shall soon be at an end, and thou shalt be rich to all the intents of bliss. Wait awhile; that weary head shall soon be girt with a crown. Stay awhile; that horny hand of labour shall soon grasp the palm branch. Wipe away that tear; God shall soon wipe away thy tears for ever. Take away that sigh—why sigh when the everlasting song is almost on thy lip? The portals of heaven stand wide open for thee. A few winged hours must fly; a few more billows must roll o'er thee, and thou wilt be safely landed on the golden shore. Do not say: " I shall be lost; I shall be cast away." Impossible.

> " Whom once he loves he never leaves,
> But loves them to the end."

If he hath called thee, nothing can divide thee from his love. The wolf of famine cannot gnaw the bond; the fire of persecution cannot burn the link, the hammer of hell cannot break the chain; old time cannot devour it with rust, nor eternity dissolve it with all its ages. Oh! believe that thou art secure; that voice which called thee, shall call thee yet again from earth to heaven, from death's dark gloom to immortality's un-uttered splendours. Rest assured, the heart that called thee beats with infinite love towards thee, a love undying, that many waters cannot quench, and that floods cannot drown. Sit thee down; rest in peace; lift up thine eye of hope and sing thy song with fond anticipation. Thou shalt soon be with the glorified, where thy portion is; thou art only waiting here to be made meet for the inheritance, and that done, the wings of angels shall waft thee far away to the mount of peace and joy and blessedness, where—

> " Far from a world of grief and sin,
>   With God eternally shut in,"

thou shalt rest for ever and ever. Examine yourselves then whether you have been called.—And may the love of Jesus be with you. Amen.

The Minister's Farewell[1]

"Wherefore I take you to record this day, that I am pure
from the blood of all men. For I have not shunned to declare unto you all the counsel of God."—Acts xx. 26, 27.

WHEN Paul was parting from his Ephesian friends, who had
come to bid him farewell at Miletus, he did not ask of them a
commendation of his ability; he did not request of them a
recommendation for his fervid eloquence, his profound learning, his comprehensive thought, or his penetrating judgment.
He knew right well that he might have credit for all these, and
yet be found a castaway at last. He required a witness which
would be valid in the court of heaven, and of value in a dying
hour. His one most solemn adjuration is: "I take you to
record this day, that I am pure from the blood of all men. For
I have not shunned to declare unto you all the counsel of
God." In the apostle this utterance was no egotism; it was a
fact that he had, without courting the smiles or fearing the
frowns of any, preached the truth, the whole truth, and nothing but the truth, as it had been taught to him by the Holy
Spirit, and as he had received it in his own heart. O that all
ministers of Christ could honestly challenge the like witness!

Now, this morning I propose, by the help of God's Spirit, to
do two things. The first will be to say a little upon *the
apostle's solemn declaration at parting*; and then, afterwards,
in a few solemn words, to *take my own personal farewell.*

I. In the first place, THE APOSTLE'S WORD AT PARTING: "I
call you to record I have not shunned to declare unto you all
the counsel of God." The first thing that strikes us is the
declaration of the apostle concerning *the doctrines he had
preached*. He had preached ALL the counsel of God. By
which I think we are to understand that he had given to his
people the entire gospel. He had not dwelt upon some one
doctrine of it, to the exclusion of the rest; but it had been his
honest endeavour to bring out every truth according to the
analogy of faith. He had not magnified one doctrine into a

[1] Sunday morning, December 11th, 1859.

6

mountain, and then diminished another into a molehill; but he had endeavoured to present all blended together, like the colours in the rainbow, as one harmonious and glorious whole. Of course, he did not claim for himself any infallibility as a man, although as an inspired man he was without error in his writings. He had, doubtless, sins to confess in private, and faults to bemoan before God. He had, doubtless, sometimes failed to put a truth as clearly as he could have wished, when preaching the Word; he had not always been as earnest as he could desire; but at least he could claim this, that he had not wilfully kept back a single part of the truth as it is in Jesus.

Now, I must bring down the apostle's saying to these modern times; and I take it, if any one of us would clear our conscience by delivering the whole counsel of God, we must take care that we preach in the first place the *doctrines of the gospel*. We ought to declare that grand doctrine of the Father's love towards his people from before all worlds. His sovereign choice of them, his covenant purposes concerning them, and his immutable promises to them, must all be uttered with trumpet tongue. Coupled with this the true evangelist must never fail to set forth the beauties of the person of Christ, the glory of his offices, the completeness of his work, and above all, the efficacy of his blood. Whatever we omit, this must be in the most forcible manner proclaimed again and again. That is no gospel which has not Christ in it, and the modern idea of preaching THE TRUTH instead of Christ, is a wicked device of Satan. Nor is this all, for as there are Three Persons in the Godhead, we must be careful that they all have due honour in our ministry. The Holy Spirit's work in regeneration, in sanctification and in perseverance, must be always magnified from our pulpit. Without his power our ministry is a dead letter, and we cannot expect his arm to be made bare unless we honour him day by day.

Upon all these matters we are agreed, and I therefore turn to points upon which there is more dispute, and consequently more need of honest avowal, because more temptation to concealment. To proceed then: I question whether we have preached the whole counsel of God, unless predestination with all its solemnity and sureness be continually declared—unless election be boldly and nakedly taught as being one of the

truths revealed of God. It is the minister's duty, beginning
from this fountain head, to trace all the other streams; dwell-
ing on effectual calling, maintaining justification by faith, in-
sisting upon the certain perseverance of the believer, and de-
lighting to proclaim that gracious covenant in which all these
things are contained, and which is sure to all the chosen, blood-
bought seed. There is a tendency in this age to throw doctrinal truth into the shade. Too many preachers are offended
with that stern truth which the Covenanters held, and to
which the Puritans testified in the midst of a licentious age.
We are told that the times have changed: that we are to
modify these old (so-called) Calvinistic doctrines, and bring
them down to the tone of the times; that, in fact, they need di-
lution, that men have become so intelligent that we must pare
off the angles of our religion, and make the square into a circle
by rounding off the most prominent edges. Any man who
doth this, so far as my judgment goes, does not declare the
whole counsel of God. The faithful minister must be plain,
simple, pointed, with regard to these doctrines. There must
be no dispute about whether he believes them or not. He
must so preach them that his hearers will know whether he
preaches a scheme of freewill, or a covenant of grace—whether
he teaches salvation by works, or salvation by the power and
grace of God.

But beloved, a man might preach all these doctrines to the
full, and yet not declare the whole counsel of God. For here
comes the labour and the battle; here it is that he who is faithful in these modern days will have to bear the full brunt of
war. It is not enough to preach doctrine; we must preach
duty, we must faithfully and firmly insist upon practice. So
long as you will preach nothing but bare doctrine, there is a
certain class of men of perverted intellect who will admire you,
but once begin to preach responsibility—say outright, once for
all, that if the sinner perish it is his own fault, that if any man
sinks to hell, his damnation will lie at his own door, and at
once there is a cry of "Inconsistency! How can these two
things stand together?" Even good Christian men are found
who cannot endure the whole truth, and who will oppose the
servant of the Lord who will not be content with a fragment,
but will honestly present the whole gospel of Christ. This is

one of the troubles that the faithful minister has to endure. But he is not faithful to God—I say it solemnly, I do not believe that any man is even faithful to his own conscience, who can preach simply the doctrine of sovereignty, and neglect to insist upon the doctrine of responsibility. I do assuredly believe that every man who sinks into hell shall have himself alone to curse for it. It shall be said of them as they pass the fiery portal: "Ye would not." "Ye would have none of my rebukes. Ye were bidden to the supper and ye would not come. I called, and ye refused; I stretched out my hands, and no man regarded. And now, behold, I will mock at your calamities. I will laugh when your fear cometh." The apostle Paul knew how to dare public opinion, and on one hand to preach the duty of man, and on the other the sovereignty of God. I would borrow the wings of an eagle and fly to the utmost height of high doctrine when I am preaching divine sovereignty. God hath absolute and unlimited power over men to do with them as he pleases, even as the potter doeth with the clay. Let not the creature question the Creator, for he giveth no account of his matters. But when I preach concerning man, and look at the other aspect of truth, I dive to the utmost depth. I am, if you will so call me, a low-doctrine man in that, for as an honest messenger of Christ I must use his own language, and cry: "He that believeth not is condemned already, because he believeth not on the Son of God." I do not see that the whole counsel of God is declared, unless those two apparently contradictory points are brought out and plainly taught. To preach the whole counsel of God it is necessary to declare the promise in all its freeness, sureness and richness. When the promise makes the subject of the text the minister should never be afraid of it. If it is an unconditional promise, he should make its unconditionality one of the most prominent features of his discourse; he should go the whole way with whatever God has promised to his people. Should the command be the subject, the minister must not flinch; he must utter the precept as fully and confidently as he would the promise. He must exhort, rebuke, command with all long-suffering. He must ever maintain the fact that the preceptive part of the gospel is as valuable—nay, as invaluable—as the promissory part. He must stand to it, that " By their fruits ye shall know them"; that "Unless the tree bring forth good fruit it is hewn down and cast into the fire." Holy living must be preached, as well as happy living. Holiness of life must be constantly insisted on, as well as that simple faith which depends for all on Christ. To declare the whole counsel of God—to gather up ten thousand things into one—I think it is needful that when a minister gets his text, he should say what that text means honestly and uprightly. Too many preachers get a text and kill it. They wring its neck, then stuff it with some empty notions and present it upon the table for an unthinking people to feed upon. That man does not preach the whole counsel of God who does not let God's Word speak for itself in its own pure, simple language. If he finds one day a text like this: "It is not of him that willeth, nor of him that runneth, but of God that sheweth mercy," the faithful minister will go all the lengths of that text. And if on the morrow the Spirit of God lays home to his conscience this: "Ye will not come unto me that ye might have life," or this other: "Whosoever will, let him come," he will be just as honest with his text on that side as he was on the other. He will not shirk the truth. He will dare to look at it straight in the face himself and then he will bring it up into the pulpit, and there say to it: "O Word, speak for thyself, and be thou heard alone. Suffer me not, O Lord, to pervert or misinterpret thine own heaven-sent truth." Simple honesty to the pure Word of God is I think requisite to the man who would not shun to declare the whole counsel of God.

Moreover, this is not all. If a man would declare the whole counsel of God, and not shun to do so, he must be very particular upon the crying sins of the times. The honest minister does not condemn sin in the mass; he singles out separate sins in his hearers, and without drawing the bow at a venture he puts an arrow on the string and the Holy Spirit sends it right home to the individual conscience. He who is true to his God does not look to his congregation as a great mass, but as separate individuals, and he endeavours to adapt his discourse to men's consciences, so that they will perceive he speaks of them. It is said of Rowland Hill, that he was so personal a preacher, that if a man were far away sitting in a window, or in some secret corner, he would nevertheless feel—"That man is speaking to me." And the true preacher who declares the whole counsel of God, so speaks, that his hearers feel that there is something for them; a reproof for their sins, an exhortation which they ought to obey, a something which comes pointedly, pertinently and personally home. Nor do I think any man has declared the whole counsel of God, who does not do this. If there be a vice that you should shun, if there be an error that you should avoid, if there be a duty that you ought to fulfil, if all these things be not mentioned in the discourses from the pulpit, the minister has shunned to declare the whole counsel of God. If there be one sin that is rife in the neighbourhood, and especially in the congregation, should the minister avoid that particular vice in order to avoid offending you, he has been untrue to his calling, dishonest to his God. I do not know how I can describe the man who declares the whole counsel of God better than by referring you to the epistles of St. Paul. There you have the doctrine and the precept, experience and practice. He tells of corruption within and temptation without. The whole divine life is portrayed, and the needed directions given. There you have the solemn rebuke, and the gentle comfort. There you have the words that "drop as the rain, and distil as the dew," and there you have the sentences that roll like thunders, and flash like lightning. There you see him at one time with his crook in his hand, gently leading his sheep into the pastures; and, anon, you see him with his sword drawn, doing valiant battle against the enemies of Israel. He who would be faithful, and preach the whole counsel of God, must imitate the apostle Paul, and preach as *he* wrote.

The question, however, is suggested, is there any temptation which arises to the man who endeavours to do this? Is there anything which would tempt him from the straight path and induce him not to preach the whole counsel of God? Ah, my brother, little do you understand the minister's position, if you have not sometimes trembled for him. Espouse but one phase of the truth, and you shall be cried up to the very heavens. Become such a Calvinist that you shut your eyes to one half the Bible, and cannot see the responsibility of the sinner, and men will clap their hands, and cry Hallelujah! and on the backs of many you shall be hoisted to a throne, and become a

very prince in their Israel. On the other hand, begin to
preach mere morality, practice without doctrine, and you shall
be elevated on other men's shoulders; you shall, if I may use
such a figure, ride upon these asses into Jerusalem; and you
shall hear them cry, Hosanna! and see them wave their palm
branches before you. But once preach the whole counsel of
God, and you shall have both parties down upon you; one
crying, "The man is too high," the other saying, "No, he is
too low"; the one will say, "He's a rank Arminian," the other,
"He's a vile hyper-Calvinist." Now, a man does not like to
stand between two fires. There is an inclination to please one
or other of the two parties, and so, if not to increase one's
adherents, at least to get a more ferociously attached people.
Ay, but if we once begin to think of that, if we suffer the cry
of either party on either hand to lead us from that narrow path
—the path of right and truth and rectitude, it is all over with
us then. How many ministers feel the influence of persons of
wealth. The minister in his pulpit, perhaps, is inclined to
think of the squire in his green pew. Or else he thinks:
"What will deacon so-and-so say?" or, "What will the other
deacon say, who thinks the very reverse?" or, "What will Mr.
A, the editor of such a newspaper, write next Monday?" or,
"What will Mrs. B say the next time I meet her?" Yes, all
these things cast their little weight into the scale; and they
have a tendency, if a man be not kept right by God the Holy
Spirit, to make him diverge a little from that narrow path, in
which alone he can stand if he would declare the whole counsel of God. Ah, friends, there are honours to be had by the
man who will espouse the opinion of a clique; but while there
are honours, there are far more dishonours to be gained by
him who will stand firm to the unstained banner of truth,
singly and alone, and do battle against mischief of every shape,
as well in the church as in the world. Therefore, it was no
mean testimony that the apostle asked for himself, that he had
not shunned to declare the whole counsel of God.

But, then, let me remark further, while there is this temptation not to declare all the counsel of God, the true minister of
Christ feels impelled to preach the whole truth, because it and
it alone can meet the wants of man. What evils has this
world seen through a distorted, mangled, man-moulded gospel.

What mischiefs have been done to the souls of men by men who have preached only one part and not all the counsel of God! My heart bleeds for many a family where Antinomian doctrine has gained the sway. I could tell many a sad story of families dead in sin, whose consciences are seared as with a hot iron, by the fatal preaching to which they listen. I have known convictions stifled and desires quenched by the soul-destroying system which takes manhood from man and makes him no more responsible than an ox. I cannot imagine a more ready instrument in the hands of Satan for the ruin of souls than a minister who tells sinners that it is not their duty to repent of their sins or to believe in Christ, and who has the arrogance to call himself a gospel minister, while he teaches that God hates some men infinitely and unchangeably for no reason whatever but simply because he chooses to do so. O my brethren! may the Lord save you from the voice of the charmer, and keep you ever deaf to the voice of error.

Even in Christian families, what evil will a distorted gospel produce! I have seen the young believer, just saved from sin, happy in his early Christian career, and walking humbly with his God. But evil has crept in, disguised in the mantle of truth. The finger of partial blindness was laid upon their eyes, and but one doctrine could be seen. Sovereignty was seen, but not responsibility. The minister once beloved was hated; he who had been honest to preach God's Word, was accounted as the off-scouring of all things. And what became the effect? The very reverse of good and gracious. Bigotry usurped the place of love; bitterness lived where once there had been a loveliness of character. I could point you to innumerable instances where harping upon any one peculiar doctrine has driven men to excess of bigotry and bitterness. And when a man has once come there, he is ready enough for sin of any kind to which the devil may please to tempt him. There is a necessity that the whole gospel should be preached, or else the spirits, even of Christians, will become marred and maimed. I have known men diligent for Christ, labouring to win souls with both hands; and on a sudden they have espoused one particular doctrine and not the whole truth, and they have subsided into lethargy. On the other hand, where men have only taken the practical side of truth, and left out the doctrinal, too many professors have run over into legality; have talked as if they were to be saved by works, and have almost forgotten that grace by which they were called. They are like the Galatians; they have been bewitched by what they have heard. The believer in Christ, if he is to be kept pure, simple, holy, charitable, Christ-like, is only to be kept so by a preaching of the whole truth as it is in Jesus. And as for the salvation of sinners, ah, my hearers, we can never expect God to bless our ministry for the conversion of sinners unless we preach the gospel as a whole. Let me get but one part of the truth, and always dwell upon it, to the exclusion of every other, and I cannot expect my Master's blessing. If I preach as he would have me preach, he will certainly own the word; he will never leave it without his own living witness. But let me imagine that I can improve the gospel, that I can make it consistent, that I can dress it up and make it look finer, I shall find that my Master is departed, and that Ichabod is written on the walls of the sanctuary. How many there are kept in bondage through neglect of gospel invitations. They are longing to be saved. They go up to the house of God, crying to be saved, and there is nothing but predestination for them. On the other hand, what multitudes are kept in darkness through practical preaching. It is do! do! do! and nothing but do! and the poor souls come away and say: " Of what use is that to me? I can do nothing. Oh, that I had a way shown to me available for salvation." Of the apostle Paul we think it may be truly said, that no sinner missed a comfort from his keeping back Christ's cross; that no saint was bewildered in spirit from his denying the bread of heaven and withholding precious truth; that no practical Christian became so practical as to become legal, and no doctrinal Christian became so doctrinal as to become unpractical. His preaching was of so savoury and consistent a kind, that they who heard him, being blessed of the Spirit, became Christians indeed, both in life and spirit, reflecting the image of their Master.

I feel I cannot dwell very long upon this text. I have been so extremely unwell for the last two days, that the thoughts which I hoped to present to you in better form, have only come tumbling out of my mouth in far from an orderly manner.

II. I must now turn away from the apostle Paul to address you A VERY FEW EARNEST, SINCERE AND AFFECTIONATE WORDS BY WAY OF FAREWELL. "Wherefore I take you to record this day that I am pure from the blood of all men, for I have not shunned to declare unto you all the counsel of God." I wish not to say anything in self-commendation and praise; I will not be my own witness as to my faithfulness; but I appeal unto you, I take you to witness this day, that I have not shunned to declare unto you all the counsel of God. Often have I come into this pulpit in great weakness, and I have far more often gone away in great sorrow, because I have not preached to you as earnestly as I desired. I confess to many errors and failings, and more especially to a want of earnestness when engaged in prayer for your souls. But there is one charge which my conscience acquits me of this morning, and I think you will acquit me too, for I have not shunned to declare the whole counsel of God. If in anything I have erred, it has been an error of judgment; I may have been mistaken, but so far as I have learned the truth, I can say that no fear of public opinion, nor of private opinion, has ever turned me aside from that which I hold to be the truth of my Lord and Master. I have preached to you the precious things of the gospel. I have endeavoured to the utmost of my ability to preach grace in all its fulness. I know the preciousness of that doctrine in my own experience; God forbid that I should preach any other. If we are not saved by grace, we can never be saved at all. If from first to last the work of salvation be not in God's hands, none of us can ever see God's face with acceptance. I preach this doctrine, not from choice, but from absolute necessity, for if this doctrine be not true, then are we lost souls; your faith is vain, our preaching is vain, and we are still in our sins, and there we must continue to the end. But, on the other hand, I can say also, I have not shunned to exhort, to invite, to entreat. I have bidden the sinner come to Christ. I have been urged not to do so, but I could not resist it. With bowels yearning over perishing sinners, I could not conclude without crying: "Come to Jesus, sinner, come." With eyes weeping for sinners, I am compelled to bid them come to Jesus. It is not possible for me to dwell upon doctrine without invitation. If you come not to Christ it is not for want of calling, or be-

cause I have not wept over your sins, and travailed in birth for
the souls of men. The one thing I have to ask of you is this:
bear me witness, my hearers, bear me witness, that in this respect I am pure from the blood of all men, for I have preached
all that I know of the whole counsel of God. Have I known a
single sin which I have not rebuked? Has there been a doctrine that I have believed which I have kept back? Has there
been a part of the Word, doctrinal or experimental, which I
have wilfully concealed? I am very far from perfect, again
with weeping I confess my unworthiness; I have not served
God as I ought to do; I have not been so earnest with you as I
could desire. Now that my three years' ministry here is over,
I could have wished that I might begin again, that I might
fall on my knees before you and beseech you to regard the
things that make for your peace. But here, again, I do repeat
it, that while as to earnestness I plead guilty, yet as to truth
and honesty I can challenge the bar of God, I can challenge the
elect angels, I can call you all to witness, that I have not
shunned to declare the whole counsel of God.

It is easy enough, if one wills to do it, to avoid preaching an
objectionable doctrine, by simply passing over the texts which
teach it. If an unpleasant truth thrusts itself on you, it is not
hard to put it aside, imagining that it would disturb your pre-
vious teaching. Such concealment may, for a while succeed,
and possibly your people will not find it out for years. But if
I have studied after anything, I have sought always to bring
out that truth which I have neglected beforehand; and if there
has been any one truth that I have kept back hitherto, it shall
be my earnest prayer that from this day forth it may be made
more prominent, that so it may be the better understood and
seen. Well, I simply ask you this question, and if I indulge in
some little egotism, if on this parting day " I am become a
fool in glorying "; it is not for the sake of glorying, it is with a
better motive—my hearer, I put this question to you. There
may come sad disasters to many of you. In a little time some
of you may be frequenting places where the gospel is not
preached. You may embrace another and a false gospel. I
only ask this thing of you: Bear me witness that it was not my
fault—that I have been faithful and have not shunned to declare unto you the whole counsel of God. In a little time some

here who have been restrained by the fact of having attended a place of worship, seeing the chosen minister has gone, may not go anywhere else afterwards. You may become careless. Perhaps next Sabbath day you may be sitting at home, lolling about and wasting the day. But there is one thing I should like to say before you make up your mind not to attend the house of God again: Bear me witness that I have been faithful with you. It may be that some here who have professedly run well for a time while they have been hearing the Word, may go back; some of you may go right into the world again; you may become drunkards, swearers and the like. God forbid that it be so! But I charge you, if you plunge into sin, do at least say this one thing for him who desires nothing so much as to see you saved—say, I have been honest with you; that I have not shunned to declare the whole counsel of God. Oh, my hearers, some of you in a little time will be on your dying-beds. When your pulse is feeble, when the terrors of grim death are round about you, if you are still unconverted to Christ, there is one thing I shall want you to add to your last will and testament; it is this—the exclusion of the poor minister who stands before you this day from any share in that desperate folly of yours which has led you to neglect your own soul. Oh, have I not cried to you to repent? Have I not bidden you look to it ere death surprised you? Have I not exhorted you, my hearers, to flee for a refuge to the hope set before you? Oh, sinner, when thou art wading through the black river, cast back no taunt on me as though I was thy murderer, for in this thing I can say: "I wash my hands in innocency; I am clear of your blood." But the day is coming when we shall all meet again. This great assembly shall be submerged into a greater, as the drop loses itself in the ocean. And I shall stand on that day to take my trial at God's bar. If I have not warned you, I have been an unfaithful watchman, and your blood will be required at my hands; if I have not preached Christ to you, and bidden you flee for refuge, then, though you perish, yet shall your soul be required of me. I beseech you, if you laugh at me, if you reject my message, if you despise Christ, if you hate his gospel, if you will be damned, yet at least give me an acquittal of your blood. I see some before me who do not often hear me; and yet I can say concerning them, they have been the subject of my private prayers; and often, too, of my tears, when I see them going on in their iniquities. Well, I do ask this one thing, and as honest men you cannot deny it me. If you will have your sins, if you will be lost, if you will not come to Christ, at least, amid the thunders of the great day, when I stand for trial at God's bar, acquit me of having destroyed your souls.

What can I say more? How shall I plead with you? Had I an angel's tongue, and the heart of the Saviour, then would I plead; but I cannot say more than I have often done. In God's name I beseech you flee to Christ for refuge. If all hath not sufficed before, let this suffice thee now. Come, guilty soul, and flee away to him whose wide open arms are willing to receive every soul that fleeth to him with penitence and faith. In a little time the preacher himself will lie stretched upon his bed. A few more days of solemn meeting, a few more sermons, a few more prayers, and I think I see myself in yon upper chamber, with friends watching around me. He who has preached to thousands now needs consolation for himself. He who has cheered many in the article of death is now passing through the river himself. My hearers, shall there be any of you whom I shall see upon my death bed who shall curse me with being unfaithful? Shall these eyes be haunted with the visions of men whom I have amused, and interested, but into whose hearts I have never sought to plunge the truth? Shall I lie there, and shall these mighty congregations pass in dreary panorama before me, and as they subside before my eyes, one after the other, shall each one curse me as being unfaithful? God forbid. I trust you will do me this favour: that when I lie a-dying you will allow that I am clear of the blood of all men, and have not shunned to declare the whole counsel of God. I see myself standing at the last great day a prisoner at the bar. What if this shall be read against me: "Thou hast had many to listen to thee; thousands have crowded to hear the words which fell from thy lips; but thou hast misled, thou hast deceived, thou hast wilfully mistaught this people." Thunders such as have been never heard before must roll over this poor head, and lightnings more terrific than have ever scathed the fiend shall blast this heart, if I have been unfaithful to you. My position—if I had but once preached the Word to these crowds, not to speak of many thousands of times—my position were the most awful in the whole universe if. I were unfaithful. Oh may God avert that worst of ills—unfaithfulness—from my head. Now, as here I stand, I make this my last appeal: "I pray you in Christ's stead be ye reconciled to God." But if ye will not be, I ask you this single favour—and I think you will not deny it me—take the blame of your own ruin, for I am pure from the blood of all men, since I have not shunned to declare unto you all the counsel of God.

This much by way of calling you to witness. Now, I come to put up a request. I have a favour to ask of all here present. If in aught you have been profited, if in anything you have ever had comfort, if you have found Christ in any way during the preaching of the gospel here, I beg you, even though you should not listen to my words again, I beg you to carry me up in your heart before the throne of God in prayer. It is by the prayers of our people that we live. God's ministers owe more to the prayers of their people than they ever know. I love my people for their prayerfulness for me. Never minister was so much prayed for as I have been. But will those of you who will be compelled to separate from us by reason of distance, and the like, will you still carry me in your thoughts before God, and let my name be engraven on your bosoms as often as you present yourselves before the mercy seat. It is a little thing I ask. It is simply that you say: "Lord, help thy servant to win souls to Christ." Ask that he may be made more useful than he has ever been; that if he is in aught mistaken he may be set right. If he has not comforted you, ask that he may do so in the future; but if he has been honest with you, then pray that your Master may have him in his holy keeping. And while I ask you to put up this request for me, it is for all those that preach the truth in Jesus. Brethren, pray for us. We would labour for you as those that must give account. Ah, it is no little thing to be a minister if we are true to our calling. As Baxter once said, when someone told him the ministry was easy work: "Sir, I wish you would take my place, if you think so, and try it." If to agonize with God in prayer, if to wrestle for the souls of men, if to be abused and not to reply, if to suffer all manner of rebukes and slanders, if this be rest, take it, sir, for I shall be glad to get rid of it. I do ask that you would pray for all ministers of Christ, that they may be helped and upheld, maintained and supported, that their strength may be equal to their day.

And, then, having put up this request for myself, and therefore a selfish one, I have an entreaty to put up for others. My hearers, I cannot shut my eyes to the fact, that there are still many of you who have long listened to the Word here, but who have still not given your hearts to Christ. I am glad to see you here, even though it should be for the last time. If you should never tread the hallowed courts of God's house again, never hear his Word, never listen to hearty invitation or honest warning, I have one entreaty to put up for you. Mark, not a request, but an entreaty; and such a one, that if I were begging for my life I could not be more honest and intensely earnest about it. Poor sinner, stop awhile, and think. If thou hast heard the gospel and not been profited by it, what wilt thou think of all thy lost opportunities when thou art on thy dying bed? What wilt thou think when thou art cast into hell, when this thought shall come ringing in thy ears: " Thou didst hear the gospel, but thou didst reject it "; when the devils in hell shall laugh in thy face, and say: " We never rejected Christ, we never despised the Word," and they shall thrust thee into a deeper hell than ever they themselves experienced. I entreat thee, stop, and think of this. Are the joys that thou hast in this world worth living for? Is not this world a dull and dreary place? Man, turn over a fresh leaf. I tell thee, there is no joy for thee here, and there is none hereafter whilst thou art what thou art. Oh, may God teach thee that the mischief lies in thy sin. Thou hast unforgiven sin about thee. As long as thy sin is unforgiven, thou canst neither be happy here, nor in the world to come. My entreaty is, go to thy chamber; if thou knowest thy self to be guilty, make a full confession there before God; ask him to have mercy upon thee, for Jesus' sake. And he will not deny thee. Man, he will not deny thee; he will answer thee; he will put all thy sins away; he will accept thee; he will make thee his child. And as thou shalt be more happy here, so shalt thou be blessed in the world to come. Oh, Christian men and women, I entreat you, implore the Spirit of God to lead many in this crowd to full confession, to real prayer, and humble faith; and if they have never repented before, may they now turn to Christ. Oh, sinner, thy life is short, and death is hastening. Thy sins are many, and if judgment has leaden feet, yet has it a sure and heavy hand. Turn, turn, turn, I beseech thee. May the Holy Spirit turn thee. Lo, Jesus is lifted up before thee now. By his five wounds, I beseech thee, turn. Look thou to him and live. Believe on him and thou shalt be saved, for whosoever believeth on the Son of Man hath everlasting life, and he shall never perish, neither shall the wrath of God rest upon him.

May the Spirit of God now command his own abiding blessing, even life for evermore, for Jesus' sake. Amen.

At the commencement of the service, MR. SPURGEON said: " The service of this morning will partake very much of the character of a farewell discourse and a farewell meeting. However sorrowful it is to me to part with many of you, whose faces I have so long seen in the throng of my hearers, yet for Christ's sake, for the sake of consistency and truth, we are compelled to withdraw from this place, and on next Sabbath morning hope to worship God in Exeter Hall. On two occasions before, as our friends are aware, it was proposed to open this place in the evening, and I was then able to prevent it by the simple declaration, that if so I should withdraw. That declaration suffices not at this time; and you can therefore perceive that I should be a craven to the truth, that I should be inconsistent with my own declarations, that in fact, my name would cease to be SPURGEON, if I yielded. I neither can nor will give way in anything in which I know I am right; and in the defence of God's holy Sabbath, the cry of this day is, ' Arise, let us go hence!' "